HOW TO RAISE A HEALTHY ACHIEVER

HOW TO RAISE A HEALTHY ACHIEVER

ESCAPING THE TYPE A TREADMILL

Laurel Hughes

ABINGDON PRESS
Nashville

HOW TO RAISE A HEALTHY ACHIEVER

Copyright © 1991 by Laurel Hughes

This book is printed on recycled, acid-free paper.

Library of Congress Cataloging-in-Publication Data

Hughes, Laurel, 1952-
  How to raise a healthy achiever :   escaping the type A treadmill / Laurel Hughes.
     p.   cm.
  Includes bibliographical references and index.
  ISBN 0-687-17929-7 (alkaline paper)
    1. Parent and child—United States.   2. Child rearing—United States.
  3. Type A behavior—United States.   I. Title.
  HQ755.85.H82   1991
  649'.1—dc20   91-8787
                                                                                    CIP

MANUFACTURED IN THE UNITED STATES OF AMERICA

Dedicated to my dad,
Spence Chamberlain,
*who showed me doing for
the joy of doing*

Contents

Acknowledgments
1. The Case of Jimmy D..13
2. The Unhealthy Achiever..................................23
3. Type **A** Parent—Type **A** Child....................37
4. Becoming a Healthy Achiever.............................51
5. Healing the Parent...71
6. Helping the Child...95
7. Western Culture and Childrearing......................113
8. Epilogue..129
   Notes..137
   Index..141

Acknowledgments

My process of writing this book was enhanced by the many fellow sojourners who took the time to share their thoughts and expertise during the course of its development. Special thanks to H. Stanton Thatcher, Psy.D., for his thorough and sensitive feedback and encouragement during the earliest version of this manuscript. Thanks also to Lee Doppelt, Ph.D.; Don Lange, Ph.D.; Janice RoggenKamp, Ph.D.; Gene Stainbrook, Ph.D.; John Thickins, M.A.; and George Zgourides, Psy.D. for their input.

The gang out at PSC-West provided much-needed moral support and encouragement as I poured myself into various stages of this endeavor; I am also grateful for living proof of the up-side of herd instinct. Special thanks to Mollie Rickard and Joe Balsamo for their companionship, *gemütlichkeit*, and continuing the legacy of "this too will pass."

And, of course, thanks to Bill, Frank, Ben, and Bridie for their continued patience and unconditional support; for providing the basis of my joy and the meaning in all that I pursue.

HOW TO RAISE A HEALTHY ACHIEVER

Chapter One

The Case of Jimmy D.

Jimmy D. was a moody child. He had plenty of playmates and did well in school, but his day-to-day living felt incomplete. He pushed harder to get better grades in school, for which he received the praise of his teachers. He increased his sphere of social influence by striving to win new friends and competing toward being a leader among his peers, and he was successful in these efforts. Yet, something was missing.

His parents seemed to be impressed by his achievements. At least, they would refrain from berating him for lack of effort if he succeeded in winning a competition or earning some high award. However, he noticed that if his report card showed six A's and one B, they would murmur only brief comments of approval for the A's. They would then go into a half-hour discussion concerning why Jimmy D. earned only a B for one class. He soon learned to doubt that his achievements were sufficient.

"Perhaps I need to change what I work toward," he pondered. "Perhaps I should find things to do that my parents seem to care about."

Jimmy D.'s father, Joe, was a small-business owner who

had worked his way up from a heritage of blue-collar workers. He still put in long hours at work, even though his business was successfully launched and thriving, so he did not have much time for family or other outside activities. In spite of his orientation toward working, Joe had always held an additional fascination for racquetball. When Jimmy D. showed some interest in finding an activity they could do together, Joe decided to enroll them both in racquetball lessons.

At first the lessons were fun. They struggled together to learn the various techniques and developed some degree of closeness as they worked together toward their common goal. As they advanced in their levels of skill, Joe decided they should compete in local tournaments. Jimmy D. was not particularly interested in competing, but he went along with it anyway, since it seemed so important to his father.

At one tournament, Jimmy D. was surprised to discover that a competitor from another club was an old friend of his from summer camp. As they waited for their turns to compete, they talked and laughed and shared "old times." As luck would have it, they were called up to compete against each other. As would be expected, the match was less than aggressive. They gingerly swatted at the ball, making a few token gestures toward scoring. When it came down to the winning point, neither of them showed any enthusiasm for coming out on top.

From the corner of his eye, Jimmy D. noticed that his father was pacing back and forth along the outside of the court. "I guess I had better do something soon," Jimmy D. decided. He made his move and scored, and was declared the winner. "Hooray!" thought Jimmy D., and he looked up at his father, in search of a sharing of his victory. Joe made eye contact with him, then sternly looked down at the floor, folded his arms, turned, and slowly walked away. Jimmy D. was crushed. During the drive home, his father maintained an icy silence, and when they arrived home, Joe let loose the fury of his indignation.

"How could you humiliate me like that!" he chastised. "After all the time we spent working toward this tournament, you put out such a paltry performance. How do you think that makes me feel? What a waste of my time! And what do you think all of those people there thought of us, with you looking so incompetent? How could you be so lazy and selfish?"

Jimmy D. was devastated. "But I've learned my lesson well," he assured himself. "Never let your friends get in the way of winning." But on a deeper level, more profound learning occurred. Jimmy D. had been given yet another piece of evidence that he just didn't measure up, at least as far as the one person who mattered most to him was concerned.

Jimmy D.'s mother, Jane, had devoted her life to encouraging her husband as he built his business and to making a home for their family. As her children grew older and her demands at home became less restrictive, she filled her time with various volunteer groups, eventually becoming involved with local politics. She was especially concerned about having the appropriate social connections and knowing about the activities of "everybody who's anybody" in their community.

Jane showed a good deal of interest in Jimmy D.'s social life as well. "You have to know the right people to get where you want to go," she encouraged. She made a point of attending all of Jimmy D.'s school performances and competitions. Afterward she would provide a critique of what could be improved upon, no matter how well Jimmy D. might have done. "Remember that you can always do better" was the motto pervading Jimmy D.'s childhood.

When Jimmy D. took Latin in high school, he met some students who seemed different from acquaintances involved with his competitive activities. The Latin students were not very popular within the social structures of the school, but he was attracted to their laid-back attitude toward one another and their ability to enthusiastically pursue common interests together. He also appreciated their ability to relax and find pleasure in studying and talking about an ancient language, or just goof off. He soon joined the Latin Club and became involved in their activities.

As he developed these friendships and increased his involvement, he wanted his mother to meet his new colleagues. One afternoon, as Jane was dropping him off for one of their meetings, he invited her to stop in and meet the club members. He especially wanted his mother to meet one of the female members—a quiet sort of girl, but he felt attracted by her kindness and good-hearted nature. His mother politely greeted each of his new friends. At home, her comments about Jimmy D.'s new friends were terse and critical.

"What a bunch of duds," she said. "Not one of them dressed as if he or she had any interest in current fashions."

Jimmy D. felt hurt by her comments, but vowed that he would not let her unreasonable disapproval interfere with his new friendships. In spite of his zeal, he soon found himself becoming less and less involved with the Latin Club. The time he spent with his new friends was marred by his memories of his mother's reaction. It was much more rewarding and pleasant when he took part in the competitive and status-oriented activities endorsed by his parents. The incident helped him nail down another important lesson as well: Appearances in life matter more than the realities that may lie beneath the surface.

Jimmy D. had been helping out in his father's hardware store since he was old enough to hold a broom. As he grew older, Joe gave him more and more tasks and responsibilities so that Joe could invest his own time in finding ways to increase his business. Jimmy D. always did the very best job he could, in the hope of finding his father's approval. But, except for the initial time Joe spent showing Jimmy D. how he wanted him to perform a new task, Jimmy D. felt his father pretty much ignored him.

"Maybe I need to show a little extra initiative," he thought, "a little extra creativity. Dad spends so much time looking for ways to make this store more successful. Maybe he would take notice if I did something that might help sales."

He settled on the idea of redoing the gardening supply displays. He spent several days taking inventory, measuring shelf space, and drawing out possible arrangements of merchandise. He wanted to surprise Joe with the changes, so he decided to rearrange the display on the day Joe had planned to stay in the back office and figure out his end-of-the-year tax forms. Between customers, Jimmy D. worked hard on the display all day. When he was finished, he called his father out in order to show him his masterpiece.

Of course, teenaged boys are still in the learning process when it comes to taking into account all of the relevant information when making plans. Jimmy D. had indeed created a very attractive and appealing display. However, it was hopelessly impractical in terms of such basics as stability, customers' being able to reach what they want, and having room to walk around it.

"What in the world do you call this?" Joe exploded. "Here I've been working my tail off all day on those idiotic tax forms, and all you can do is find ways of making more work for me so I can't get them done. This is my store, and things will be done my way. What makes you think a punk like you can just come in and do whatever you please?"

The tirade continued for several minutes, ending when Jimmy D. took off his apron, threw it on the floor, yelled "I quit!" and stormed out of the store.

"I'll show him!" Jimmy D. fumed. "Who needs him? I can do as well or better than he can, and I can prove it."

Since it was Jimmy D.'s senior year, he had applied to several different universities. His good grades and excellent records paid off: He was offered scholarships by several schools. But instead of enrolling at the university known for its fine program in business administration, which his father had been pressuring him to pursue, he enrolled at a prestigious institute of technology, where he began a course of studies toward an engineering degree.

Jimmy D.'s courses were difficult, but he had always been a hard worker and was prepared for the challenge. He tried out for sports and became involved in school politics with the same fervor he had in high school. He joined a fraternity and dated only sorority members, which was how he met his future wife, Joanna. She dropped out of school during her senior year in order to get a job and help finance the remainder of Jimmy D.'s education.

They married after he graduated and moved to a nearby suburb, where Jimmy D. had landed an excellent position in an electronics firm. They bought a nice home in a prestigious neighborhood and were able to finance the acquisition of two expensive foreign cars. They had two children—Joey and Janet—and were able to send them to the best private school in the area. Jimmy D. was respected at his job for his hard-working attitude and his penchant for excellence, although he was also known for being a little temperamental.

It would appear that Jimmy D. had it all. But he was not happy. No matter how much he accomplished, there were always other goals he felt he must reach or tasks he must perform before he could feel satisfied with himself. There were so many things he wanted to do, but he just never seemed to find the time. He felt frustrated and incompetent because of his inability to expand the number of his life pursuits. He crammed more and more activities into less and less time as he tried to maximize the use of his waking hours. He slowly increased the hours he spent at work and decreased the amount of time spent at home. He had no difficulty justifying the time he spent away from his family, since he certainly couldn't work at home with all of the distractions going on around him.

Pressures to perform became enormous. He occasionally tried out a new sport or physical activity to work off some of the stress, but he never persevered for long. Exercise seemed to be just one more thing that took up time, and he had nothing to show for it when he was finished. If the pressure became too great, he would unwind with a highball or two instead.

Jimmy D.'s physician continually warned him to slow down and take care of himself, but with little success. He was concerned about Jimmy D.'s blood pressure and the impact of his hair-trigger temper on his cardiovascular system.

Joanna was not happy, either. She enjoyed all that Jimmy D. had provided for her, and she appreciated the freedom she had to take part in activities of her own choosing, since there was no need for her to find an outside job. But she was lonely. During the rare occasions when Jimmy D. was home, he was either asleep on the couch or curled up with a drink in front of the television set. If Joanna would try to draw him into a conversation, he would become angry.

"Haven't I earned a little time to myself?" he would retort to her complaints. "You sound just like my parents. Nothing I do is ever good enough."

"It's not a question of being good enough," she would explain. "I just want to feel as if you still care about me. We never just talk. And it seems that you hardly ever touch me or hold me."

"Oh, come on. I touched you plenty the other night."

"That's not what I meant," she would say. "I'm not talking about sex. I want affection. I want to feel loved. And it's hard for me to feel loved when you're always blowing up at me or the kids."

"How can you question that I love you? Why do you think I work so hard in the first place? I've given you and the kids a better life-style than either of our families were able to provide for us. What more do you want?"

Eventually Joanna would retreat into a cocoon of frustration, and, on the surface, Jimmy D. would feel justified in his attitude. He was aware that he didn't show much physical affection to his family, but then neither did his parents, and they had still managed to stay together all this time. So what if he used his anger to get his family to shape up? That's what his father had done, and it hadn't hurt him any.

But each time he was confronted with Joanna's dissatisfaction, he would be left feeling inadequate. Here was just one more way that he didn't measure up. As an attempt to balm over these feelings, he drove himself to achieve even more, in the hope of somehow proving his adequacy. And the more Joanna would plead for attention, the more he closed himself off from her and others. "Who needs this pain?" he would grumble.

Joanna wondered about herself as she interacted with her husband. She wanted to feel loved, but she recognized that Jimmy D. had to feel happy before he could provide affection of any sort. "If I can make our home life pleasing for him, maybe then he will be more affectionate," she hypothesized.

Joanna went out of her way to make sure that Joey and Janet behaved in ways that would not set off Jimmy D.'s impatient outbursts. She kept the house spotless and restricted the children's activities so that the main living areas would suit Jimmy D.'s agenda. He would occasionally tolerate input from others, but Joanna allowed him to maintain almost total control over all final decisions. He even dictated which leisure activities the children should participate in, no matter what their desires might be. Joanna supported his agenda, since to challenge him would mean enduring another angry blow up. She encouraged the children to do well in their pursuits, since she knew that Jimmy D. would interpret their failings as his own personal failure, which would result in even more episodes of unpleasantness.

Thus the years went by, with Joanna and the children desperately attempting to be the perfect family that Jimmy D. could love. And Jimmy D. continued to push himself to achieve more and more, in the hope of finally accomplishing enough to bolster his faltering feelings of self-worth. Of course, the magic number of achievements and his degree of desired perfection were never reached. This merry-go-round came to a grinding halt with Jimmy D.'s almost fatal heart attack, resulting in his having a lengthy hospital stay.

Right after the attack, Jimmy D. felt a sense of relief. As he lay in bed, incapacitated and hooked up to various tubes and apparatuses, he shared this with Joanna: "You know, I don't think I ever could have slowed down without something like this happening," he considered out loud. "I felt so pressured to perform, to be the best, and to have it all. I never could have stopped myself."

Joanna supported him as he worked his way toward recovery. He threw himself into rehabilitation with the same "full steam ahead" and perfectionism he had used to motivate himself throughout his life. Before long he was almost as good as new. However, his doctor warned him that he could not continue to live the life-style he had lived before and still expect to stay alive. Jimmy D. heeded his advice and vowed that he would do better. But soon after he had gotten back into the swing of things, he found himself pushing toward achievement in the same way he had always done. He recognized what he was doing to himself, but he found ways to justify ignoring the significance of the potential effects of his behavior.

"Is life really worth living if I have no value in this world?" he rationalized. "Unless I can achieve and have something to offer, I have no reason to exist."

Joey and Janet had been badly frightened by the near loss of their father. Joey, then a teenager, was particularly affected. The possibility of becoming "the man of the house" had loomed large before him, a role for which he was not yet prepared. He had picked up a lot of the slack left in household functioning while his father was in the hospital and maintained some extra duties while Jimmy D. rehabilitated.

One day while Joey was mowing the front lawn, he noticed a large rock hiding beneath the grass. "Boy, I'm glad I spotted that," he thought. "Dad would kill me if I bent up the mower blades on it."

Rather than stop the mower to pick up the rock, he decided to pick it up as he passed by, for the purpose of taking less time. As he grabbed at it, he found that it was somewhat lodged in the ground. He let go of the mower so he could use both hands. The mower, being self-propelled, continued on without him. It proceeded down the bank, mowing a large bare strip through the alyssum beds before Joey caught up with it.

Jimmy D. could not believe his eyes when he saw what Joey had done to the front yard. "How could anyone do something so careless!" he bellowed. "What are the neighbors going to think, that I raised an idiot for a son?"

Joey could not bear the force of his father's anger and disapproval.

"Forget you!" he yelled. He jumped on his bike and pedaled off down the road as fast as he could, with tears of anguish streaming down his cheeks. "I'll show him," he fumed. . . .

Chapter Two

The Unhealthy Achiever

The story of Jimmy D. is entirely fictional. Yet, the elements involved as his life unfolded are real and, in fact, commonplace. Our culture values achievement, and this value influences how we perceive ourselves and our world, our feelings about our lives, and how we interact with our children. We want our children to grow up and have happy, productive lives, as surely were the desires of the parents in Jimmy D.'s story. But as his history so graphically illustrated, our good intentions may not influence our children in the manner we had hoped they would.

Jimmy D.'s family is an example of unhealthy achieving and how it can perpetuate itself through the generations. Not all unhealthily achieving families are identical to his. Sometimes the hard-driving parent is the mother, rather than the father, or perhaps both parents are overachievers. The underpinnings of unhealthy achieving are such that it can develop even in families in which neither parent has such an orientation, given the right set of circumstances. Many people with an overachievement orientation are not as outwardly successful as the individuals in Jimmy D.'s family. And only a minority of stress-ridden achievers develop cardiovascular disease as severe as Jimmy D.'s. The degree of severity of both physical and emotional effects of such a life-style and value system varies greatly. In fact, most families in Western society show at least a few symptoms of unhealthy achieving, just because the achievement orientation is so ingrained in our culture.

Over the last few decades, a group of creative and courageous investigators has been pioneering the study and treatment of the more severely affected unhealthy high achievers.[1] They call their constellation of achievement-related behaviors the "type A" behavior pattern. Since their early struggles to establish the recognition of this behavior pattern and its potential ill effects on the cardiovascular system, the number of studies on this topic has swelled to the point of providing some clear guidance for us as we deal with our own type A behavior.

More recently, researchers have also begun looking at children's type A behavior and the behavior of their parents.[2] Such research and its findings let us begin to consider primary prevention of type A behavior. In other words, we can begin to look at how the way we parent might affect whether we raise a healthy, happy achiever or an unhealthy type A achiever.

The exact nature of what type A behavior represents, or even what it is, has only recently come close to being specified. As I work with parents on their style of child rearing, the concept of teaching a child to achieve without becoming type A is often met with confusion. "What do you mean, a nontype A achiever? Aren't the achievement orientation and type A behavior the same thing?" No, they are not.

WHAT TYPE A BEHAVIOR LOOKS LIKE

The most noticeable characteristic of type A individuals is that they always seem to be in a hurry. They have a long list of things they want to get done, and they may in fact carry around an ever-growing written list of everything they want to accomplish in a given day. It seems as if they cram more activities into a given time slot than would be considered humanly possible to complete. One way of managing this heavy load is to do two things at once. You might notice that type A individuals often read while they eat, cook or do dishes while talking on the phone, shave or put on make-up while driving to work, and so on.

Type A persons will also move quickly and talk with a rapid pace. They will finish other people's sentences, interrupt, and respond to questions before the asker has finished the question just to keep things moving. Type A individuals drive quickly, often tailgating other vehicles and changing lanes frequently in order to make the best possible time. They seem to be constantly evaluating the fastest way to get somewhere and take a variety of shortcuts in their daily functioning for the purpose of "efficiency."

Type A persons have a terrible time with their patience and will do whatever possible to avoid waiting in lines. They might go to the store or to movies only during times when they know there will not be a crowd to contend with. They often carry around a book or some other pastime to busy themselves with just in case they do get stuck waiting somewhere. Even while they are engaged in an activity, you can observe the impatience of type A individuals when things aren't moving quickly enough for them by their finger-tapping, heavy sighing, and knee-jiggling as they try to keep themselves in a perpetual state of "progression."

Another observable characteristic of type A individuals is their apparent ongoing state of being irritated or angry, with a tendency to blow up over seemingly trivial events. This anger often shows itself when something happens that gets in the way of the type A person's goals being met.

Outbursts may seem to others unpredictable and are often decorated with liberal use of profanity.

Sometimes it seems that type A individuals design their daily living in a way that provides opportunities to become angry. They often direct conversation toward topics they can become upset about, and they become highly critical and angry about the "injustices" of the world. They form strong, fixed opinions on almost every topic and defend them to the death, no matter how ridiculous their position may begin to appear. They speak of having high ideals, but often these "ideals" seem more like fanaticism and just one more excuse to become angry or critical of others.

Often aggressiveness accompanies the type A person's reaction toward perceived sources of irritation. In the face of being contradicted by another person, or in some other way being blocked by someone else's standpoint, the type A individual may resort to put-downs, sarcasm, name calling, ridicule, getting even, and other sorts of attacks on the self-esteem or well-being of the person who is in the way of the type A person's agenda. When it comes to being sensitive to the needs or feelings of others, type A individuals appear to be oblivious to such details as they work endlessly toward their mountain of goals. Not only are they poor losers when they fail to come out on top in various forms of competition, but they are also poor winners, as they ridicule or show condescension toward the losers.

In addition to being hurried and easily angered, type A individuals do other things that suggest to the outside viewer that they are distancing themselves from the world in general. They appear as if they are constantly fighting against something, someone, or even time itself. They don't seem to enjoy the actual process of doing or living in the world. Instead, they get excited only when victories are at hand. Even then, however, they don't stop and appreciate the good feeling of having accomplished something, since they are too busy focusing on the next potential notch in their belts.

For the type A person, counting notches comes to take the place of enjoying the more qualitative experience of living. When presented with a beautiful painting, the type A person is more likely to say, "How much does it cost?" than, "Oh, how lovely." When talking to others about their occupations, type A persons ask questions like, "How much do you make?" "How many customers do you serve?" and "How much do you produce?" rather than, "How do you like your job?" "What aspects of it do you find to be satisfying (or dissatisfying)?" and "What do you do in your spare time?"

Type A people themselves don't seem to have spare time, and what few leisure activities they have do not seem to be framed within the schema of enjoyment. They may run or jog, but they do so more for the purpose of attaining "good health" than for enjoyment, as they focus on breaking their last running time, going yet a little farther than before, or running faster than their competitors. Contrast this to the person who enjoys a brisk walk in pleasant surroundings, perhaps taking along the dog or a friend with whom to converse. The concept of "stop and smell the roses" has little meaning to the type A person, who might snort, "So what would smelling roses accomplish?"

Thus far I have made repeated references to a seeming connection between type A behavior and competitiveness. Type A individuals are indeed competitive people. However, competitiveness is not an exclusively type A trait. The difference lies within how a person uses competitiveness in his or her life. For the typical type A person, the sole purpose of competing is to win. Others might compete because they enjoy winning, but in addition, they enjoy the activity itself within which they are competing. They are also more likely to enjoy the process and excitement of competition itself, whether they win or lose, and are able to enjoy seeing their fellow competitors win.

Type A individuals are usually also achievement-oriented, but a person is not necessarily type A because of his or her orientation toward achieving. Healthy achievers enjoy the process of achieving, and they can stop and bask in the glow of a recent accomplishment. They talk about their achievements with others because they feel good about them and want to share those pleasant feelings and rejoice as one with the people they are close to. The type A person, on the other hand, achieves for the purpose of coming out on top. After reaching a goal, the type A individual might utter a brief "hooray for me," but would then refocus on the next mountain to climb. When talking about successes with others, the type A's purpose is to communicate, "See how good I am (and probably better than you are)," rather than to share a good feeling.

Early research on type A behavior did not make this fine distinction, and in fact tended to lump all competitive and achievement-oriented behavior types into the type A category. As more and more information has been gathered on type A behavior, it has become clear that the various dysfunctions suffered by type A individuals are not necessarily related to competitiveness and the achievement orientation. Instead, the disorder appears to be a function of "time urgency"—the need always to hurry and accomplish as much as possible in the smallest possible amount of time—and "free-floating hostility"—the constant state of irritation or anger that type A individuals use to propel themselves toward their goals.

Because of the absence of this distinction during earlier research, the outcomes of long-term studies on the treatment of type A behavior have emerged with mixed results. Whether or not treatment is successful appears to be due at least in part to how the researchers define type A behavior. Studies that defined type A individuals as those with time urgency and free-floating hostility had a tendency to find fewer cardiovascular accidents after treatment, while those who did not take these characteristics exclusively into account did not find improvement.[3]

Unfortunately, many writers and researchers have interpreted the ambivalent findings to mean that treatment of type A behavior does not work. Perhaps a better interpretation of the data is that we are not entirely certain that treatment of type A behavior can prevent cardiovascular disease and that we will need to do a few more studies using a more appropriately defined type A population before we can know for sure. Also, perhaps avoiding cardiovascular disease should not be the only consideration we take into account as we decide whether to avoid type A behavior. The hurried, angry, interpersonally isolating life-style of the type A individual is not consistent with what most of us would envy or call "happy." The type A person may not even know what feeling happy is, outside of the brief feeling experienced immediately after some fine accomplishment. This in itself is a serious impairment in living one's daily life, and certainly should be included as part of deciding whether treatment is successful.

A goal for treatment, then, would be in some way to alter the inner functioning of type A individuals so that they do not live such half-known lives. *And our goal, as parents, is to raise our children in such a way that their inner functioning supports healthy achieving, rather than hard-driving, stress-ridden, and emotionally impaired achieving.*

WHAT GOES ON INSIDE THE TYPE A?

The bedrock lying beneath the type A personality is low self-esteem, status insecurity, or a combination of both. Are you surprised? Many people are. How could these people, who achieve so much and battle their way up to such high levels of status and power, not think well of themselves? I will reveal more about how low self-esteem and status insecurity become implanted in type A individuals in a later chapter. For now, I will explain how low self-esteem and status insecurity feed the type A behavior pattern.

Type A individuals lead the kind of lives they do as a reaction to their low self-esteem or status insecurity, learning to bolster their floundering self-esteem by using their accomplishments as an external yardstick for measuring self-worth. Rather than seeing themselves as worthwhile and valuable just because they are who they are, they define their worth according to how much they have achieved and how they compare to others' achievements.

Unfortunately, they never achieve enough to be able to feel adequate. There is always somebody who has done more or achieved higher goals than the type A person has, and it is against these individuals that the type A person compares himself or herself. Since there will always be people in the world who have achieved as much or more than the type A, he or she can never achieve the goal of coming out on top. Nevertheless, the type A person tries to achieve more and more in less and less time to try "to catch up with the competition." In this manner, the type A person develops the sense of time urgency I described earlier.

Furthermore, type A people feel pressed to dominate and control all situations, since their environmental arena serves as the medium in which they establish their worth. They must win all arguments and compete with those around them, because to "lose" or not look as competent as someone else would reflect on their perception of their worth. They try to take control over everybody and everything even vaguely connected to their lives, since only through being in control can they feel certain that nothing will happen that could somehow reflect on them.

Free-floating hostility is also a product of their low self-esteem. Type A individuals have an underlying feeling of being "emotionally slighted"—that somewhere along the line they did not get the affection or approval they needed or deserved. Their hostility is "free-floating" because it does not have an appropriate object toward which the type A person can direct it. All the type A person experiences is the constant feeling of irritation or anger, as a residue from his or her past emotional slight. The most convenient release the type A person can have from the discomfort of these feelings is to dump them on those around him or her, resulting in putdowns, sarcasm, name-calling, vengefulness, and the like. They may pedantically scrutinize their surroundings, looking for something to criticize, just so they can have an outlet for their inner turmoil. Type A individuals are likely to blow up when their goals are blocked not only because it gives them the opportunity to vent their anger, but also because the blockage is perceived as just one more "jerk" or aspect of the world that is trying to keep them from getting what they need, want, or deserve.

Type A persons carry their feeling of not having received what they needed into their current interpersonal relationships. No matter how much approval and affection are directed toward them, they focus on the times when approval and affection were absent or lacking. Thus they never feel as if they are getting enough. They tend to search for an ideal spouse who can supply them with a constant flow of love and approval. But, since nobody is perfect, spouses always fall short in the eyes of their type A partners, who selectively focus on inadequacies.

Their interpersonal lives are further impaired by their feelings of hostility and their need to dominate. Since blowing up at people and trying to dominate and control them is inconsistent with showing affection or mutual respect, type A individuals are handicapped in their ability to be on the giving side of a loving relationship. Even if they do show affection, it may not be trusted by their significant others, since from their experience they know that their type A spouse could blow up over anything at any moment. Type A individuals have difficulty experiencing joy or elation over the successes of others because they are so preoccupied with trying to be the one with the most success themselves. Other people's successes are, therefore, considered to be a threat, not something to rejoice about. This results in missed opportunities to experience true closeness with others.

Type A individuals' preoccupation with power also interferes with their getting along with others. They strive to protect themselves by dominating and controlling their surroundings. Then they feel threatened when they try to function within our various societal structures, which they tend to view as power structures rather than as responsibility structures. Type A individuals have difficulty interacting with others within the hierarchies typically found in places of employment, anything related to government, or any other socially sanctioned structure that might give someone else more power than the type A person has. They even have a difficult time sharing power within marital structures, usually demanding almost all control in decision making and becoming manipulative and punitive whenever their spouses won't let themselves be dominated. This style of handling power alienates type A individuals from other persons, which further contributes to the type A persons' feelings of inadequacy, insecurity, and loneliness.

HOW ARE TYPE A INDIVIDUALS AFFECTED PHYSICALLY?

The life-style of typical type A persons is a stressful one indeed. Their sense of time urgency, continual feelings of irritation, and nonexistent time for relaxation guarantee a constant state of anxiety. In recent years much has been written about the impact of stress on the body. Type A individuals are especially prone to feel the ill effects of stress, since they have chosen it as a life-style.

Meyer Friedman and Diane Ulmer believe that the most significant damage type A persons inflict upon their bodies concerns excess norepinephrine.[4] Norepinephrine is a hormone that the body secretes in abundance during times of stress. Type A individuals produce larger amounts of this hormone than do non-type A individuals when they are faced with difficult challenges, find that their goals are being blocked, or have found some other reason to become inordinately upset. This hormone has an impact on the cardiovascular system as it helps to regulate the functioning of the heart and large and small arteries. Friedman and Ulmer list three diseases that may be a result of this excess norepinephrine.

First, type A individuals can be prone to migraine headaches. Norepinephrine affects the dilation and constriction of the small arterial vessels that support the covering of the brain. The fluctuations in the dilation and constriction of vessels can contribute to migraine headache symptoms.

Second, type A individuals may develop high blood pressure. This is because the norepinephrine increases the rate of heart contractions and also narrows the smaller arteries throughout the body. Thus the cardiovascular system is not only trying to pump blood faster, but is also trying to do so within a more limited area, resulting in higher blood pressure.

Third, and most serious, type A individuals can develop coronary heart disease. Friedman and Ulmer suspect that the excess norepinephrine may contribute to the breakdown of the plaque that lines the inside of the three major coronary arteries. When the damaged plaque eventually ruptures, blood clots and forms a thrombus, which can eventually block the flow of blood, which nourishes the heart muscle itself. Lack of nourishment causes the afflicted part of the heart muscle to die, resulting in a heart attack. While they are still not certain of the exact process by which excess norepinephrine results in heart attacks, nonetheless many researchers observe a strong relationship between type A behavior and heart disease.

The likelihood of heart failure in type A individuals is further increased by the type of exercise they choose. Since exercise must have a competitive element before it seems worthwhile to them, type A individuals tend to choose activities like running, racquetball, handball, and other sports that show how well they can "take it." The resulting scenario goes something like this.

The type A person already has a scarred heart muscle because of the damage indirectly caused by the excess norepinephrine. However, the person is probably not aware of it, since the only sure way to find out is through the use of an angiogram (the treadmill test throws too many false negative readings to be useful in this respect). So the type A person finds some vigorous exercise to pursue that will both supposedly strengthen the heart muscle and provide a means to compete and thereby prove himself or herself. As the type A person engages in his or her activity, the already damaged heart muscle is being forced to perform at full capacity for extended periods. Remember the old Chevy with cracked rings that you (or very likely one of your cohorts) used to drag race back in high school? And do you remember what eventually happened to it? The same thing happens to type A individuals when they put excessive pressure on their cardiovascular system—they "blow their engines." More technically, the type A person pushes his or her heart beyond its ability to keep up, it goes into an irregular rhythm, and the person collapses.

WHAT HAPPENS TO TYPE A INDIVIDUALS SPIRITUALLY?

Spirituality—whether it is practiced in a traditional, organized form or is more personal and individualized—demands that we be in touch with our experiencing ability. In order to access spirituality, we need to be able to feel a sense of oneness with various aspects of our worship practices. It can take the form of feeling in tune with nature as we sense the awe of creation. We might experience it as a feeling of peace within the constructs of God's forgiveness, or the glow we find as we feel his abundant love. It can be a feeling of security as we feel cared for or protected by God or by an ultimate plan of nature. Spirituality can be felt as we worship with a group of believers within our faith, as we sense and recognize our common causes and the oneness to be shared among us.

Type A individuals are impaired in their ability to experience such feelings. The same dynamics that keep type A individuals from relating successfully with others keep them from relating with themselves or with their object of worship as well. They can't slow down long enough to appreciate spiritual feelings because they are so focused on achieving and pursuing their goals. Goals are future-oriented; spirituality involves being able to experience the present.

The type A person's basis for establishing self-worth can also get in the way of living in a manner consistent with his or her religious beliefs. Most Judeo-Christian faiths teach that we are valuable because we are valued highly by God, not because of our gifts or various "works." Type A individuals live their lives for the purpose of works, not faith, for it is through the pursuit of works that they hope to establish feelings of worth. Thus the religious type A person loses out on experiencing the self-worth that is offered fully and freely by his or her faith—no strings attached. Instead, the degree and visibility of the type A person's church involvement becomes just one more external yardstick for measuring his or her self-worth.

CONCLUSION

In summary, the type A behavior pattern is damaging emotionally, interpersonally, physically, and even spiritually. It begins with insufficient feelings of being cared for and approved of, which leads to low self-esteem, status insecurity, and free-floating hostility. The person tries to make up for the low self-esteem and status insecurity by striving toward achievement, and the free-floating hostility bursts forth when efforts toward achievement are blocked. This relentless pursuit of achievement, unrealistically competitive attitude, and the resulting hostility toward the world alienate the person from others and prevent him or her from enjoying relaxation, spirituality, and meaningful interpersonal relationships. In addition, every time the person lets loose free-floating hostility, he or she is injecting huge amounts of norepinephrine into the bloodstream, which contributes to a variety of physical ailments, including possible sudden cardiac death.

What I have described thus far is the classic, full-fledged type A behavior pattern. Most people who are type A show only some of these symptoms. We might speculate that it is the type A individual with the fuller set of symptoms who is likely to have the more severe cardiovascular problems. Nonetheless, even moderate degrees of type A behavior can be unhealthy, at the very least on emotional and interpersonal levels.

Chapter Three

Type **A** Parent—Type **A** Child

The preceding chapter describes a miserable existence, an existence that could even be cut short by an untimely death. It is not the life pattern or the consequences we think of when we joke with each other about our own type A behaviors. But perhaps this is because only recently has the true nature of type A behavior been specified and revealed. Just being competitive or enjoying achievement is not necessarily a bad state of affairs. It can be healthy and normal.

But if we never separate out possible unhealthy aspects of overachieving and competitiveness, since we are assuming that bad health just comes with the territory, chances are good that we will in some way continue to torture ourselves unnecessarily. Likewise, we might encourage the same maladaptive beliefs and behaviors within our children—not because of malice or inept abilities, but because we have not yet been able to view achievement and competitiveness within both a healthy and an unhealthy framework.

I fully and freely admit that I suffer some of the symptoms of type A behavior. The number and severity of type A symptoms I still experience are continually diminishing, as I sort out and confront these tendencies toward self-destruction. Part of my motivation for changing my life-style and belief systems is for the benefit of my own state of being. However, the thought of inflicting the same pressured life-style and potential symptomatology onto my children makes my blood run cold. "Could I be signing my children's death warrants by the way I parent?" is the question that shook me from my complacent, overly intellectualized, type A fog.

I decided that there must be a way to help protect my children from the same nightmare, as well as protect their adult health. Of course, as adults they will make their own choices, and that will be their business. My concern was that I not unknowingly and unduly influence them toward an unhealthy style of achieving, just because of my lack of awareness of how my own pathology might influence them in this way.

Having combed through the research on type A behavior, children's type A behavior, and the behavior of their parents—in addition to having held it against my background in child development—I have drawn some conclusions about how a type A parental style of interaction might affect children's potential for type A behavior. This chapter shares these conclusions as well as some hypotheses about how type A behavior can develop in children whose parents are not type A.

BUILDING THE TYPE A CORNERSTONE

In order to become a type A, the first necessity is that a child have feelings of low self-esteem and/or status insecurity. While there are many ways children can develop such feelings, the classic type A style of interaction during parenting can be especially prone to produce low self-esteem in children.

First, time urgency interactions affect children's attitudes toward themselves. Children demand a lot of time and parental attention. They are inquisitive and intrusive, and tend not to be aware of the importance parents place on their personal activities. Since type A parents cram their schedules with their own achievement-related pursuits, children can become an inconvenience. They get in the way of the goals the type A parent has set for himself or herself. As a result, type A parents often blow up at their children when they won't stay out of their hair. These blow-ups seem arbitrary to the child, who experiences the outbursts as evidence of his or her own "badness," rather than a representation of the parent's lack of patience.

Because of their tendency to interrupt and hurry conversation along, type A parents may not listen fully to what their children have to say. Children are not skilled at expressing themselves succinctly and accurately, since communication skills are learned as part of the socialization process. As a result, children may not get the whole idea out before the type A parent is cutting them off and giving them the parent's view or input. The child experiences the lack of listening as meaning that what he or she has to say can't be very important, leaving the child feeling unsupported and insecure. The restricted time type A parents spend with their children in general as they pursue their own goals leaves the children feeling that they can't be worth much.

Second, free-floating hostility in parents can affect a child's perception of his or her self-worth in a variety of ways. The type A person's liberal use of criticism does not bypass the parenting arena. Type A parents are keenly tuned to whatever shortcomings are apparent in their children's behavior, and therefore point out more of their children's failures than their successes. So the child can never perform well enough for the parent not to find something that can be improved upon. And the child learns that his or her efforts, no matter how successful, can never quite measure up. The result is low self-esteem.

The need of the type A person to always be right also plays itself out during parenting. If the type A parent always has to be "right" in a discussion or argument, then the child is always "wrong." The child eventually figures that he or she must be pretty dumb. Furthermore, the type A parent might point out the child's "wrongness" in a belittling manner, leaving the child not only feeling dumb, but also perceiving himself or herself to be a major disappointment to the parent. This further encourages low self-esteem.

Competitive games played with children must be won by the type A parent, since classic type A individuals cannot tolerate losing. So the child never gets to win, since often the only way a child can win is if the adult loses on purpose, which the type A parent is unlikely to do. Since the child, therefore, always loses, he or she does not develop feelings of competency. Even if the child wins legitimately, the type A parent then becomes disgruntled over losing, leaving the child feeling bewildered, rejected, and of little worth.

Third, the type A individual's difficulty with showing genuine affection can affect her or his child's feelings of worth. Children can perceive their type A parents' awkward attempts to show affection as being cold and insincere, which they may in fact be. When children do not feel loved by their parents, or cannot trust their showing of affection because it is interspersed with seemingly arbitrary hostilities, the children have difficulty learning how to care about or nurture themselves. Also, there is a tendency for type A parents to show sincere affection only after a child has achieved something. Thus affection and positive regard are not unconditional, as is needed for good self-esteem. These children learn instead that they are valued more for their achievements than because of any inherent self-worth.

A fourth element of parental type A behavior that has an effect on children is the parents' tendency to use virtually everything as a measure of their self-esteem. Type A parents often develop an enmeshed relationship with their children, which means that they have difficulty experiencing their children as separate individuals. They do not view their child's successes or failures purely as the child's successes or failures. Instead, they use their child's performance as a measure of their own worth. And, of course, since typical type A individuals try to take control of everything that they connect with their self-esteem, type A parents become overcontrolling with their children. They attempt to protect their self-esteem by overly coercing their child, using power-oriented styles of discipline, not being receptive to their child's ideas on how his or her life should proceed, and ultimately devaluing the child's ability to make choices and to control himself or herself. The child ends up feeling both powerless and inadequate.

In summary, type A parents can create low self-esteem in their children through their time urgency, free-floating hostility, difficulty in showing affection, and familial enmeshment. But self-esteem and self-perceived status can be diminished by a number of other childhood experiences as well. Losing a parent to divorce, illness, or death can leave a child feeling insecure or of low self-worth. Poverty and other traumatic childhood life circumstances also produce these feelings. Homes in which parents are physically, emotionally, or sexually abusive often produce children who feel of little worth. In short, any childhood experience that would give children the message that they are not of value can result in low self-esteem and status insecurity, which can in turn become the cornerstone of type A functioning.

Something else we need to keep in mind is children's innate tendencies. The latest research suggests that a good deal of our personality stems from the type of temperament with which we were born.[1] For example, some children appear to be wired more sensitively than others. A sensitive child is more likely to react to unpleasant circumstances than is a more easygoing child. Thus we might speculate that a sensitive child would be more likely to develop low self-esteem than would his or her hardier counterpart, which would make the sensitive child more likely to be drawn into the type A behavior pattern. **CAUTION:** This does not mean that type A behavior is inborn and that you're stuck with it, so why even bother to try to intervene. With the exception of a handful of reflexes, behaviors are learned, not innate. All I am pointing out here is that it is easier for some people to adopt type A behaviors than it is for others. Long-term research suggests that although some people may be wired to be more sensitive, as time goes on many learn to adapt to their environments; they teach themselves to keep their sensitivities at bay when they become maladaptive.[2] We can't change the temperaments we were born with, but we can change the way we manage them.

THE DEVELOPMENT OF FREE-FLOATING HOSTILITY

Free-floating hostility can be a by-product of the same childhood experiences that promote low self-esteem. The simplest way to describe it is that these children subconsciously or even consciously resent the fact that they did not get what was due them.

Children are fascinating examples of the natural process of growth. Rarely is it necessary to push or teach a child to be goal oriented for the child to make efforts toward learning to walk or talk, just as we don't need to teach a flower how to bloom. Children come equipped with a natural drive toward learning about their world and seeking out what works for them in it, a drive that fuels them toward growth, maturity, and self-actualization. Similar to a flower's needs, the child's growing environment needs to be an appropriate medium within which growth is possible—well-tilled, supportive soil, so that the child's roots can extend and become solid and secure; and the availability of nutrients, so that the child has the ingredients necessary for molding and developing blossoming skills and a healthy personality.

Our job as parents is to provide such an environment. It involves seeking a balance between allowing children's natural growth drive to emerge as much as possible, perhaps providing opportunity for it to do so, and at the same time providing enough structure within the children's home lives so that they can see the limits to which they can assert themselves and still function within our society. Most parents are successful in providing some form of this "average expectable environment"—an environment that both supports and guides a young child.[3]

Many aspects of type A parenting interfere with the provision of such an environment. The error can swing in both directions of the environmental pendulum: The type A parent's behavior may create such an unpredictable atmosphere that the child feels too threatened to allow his or her self-realization to emerge, or it could also be so overstructured and overcontrolled that the child's "roots" cannot find room to grow.

First, many aspects of type A behavior in parents feel uncomfortable or nonsupportive to their children. Type A parents' lack of priority in terms of spending time with their children removes a source of validation of their efforts. "Look at this, Daddy" may be met with "Not now, I'm busy," rather than "I like that," "How interesting," or any other comment that might suggest to children that their environment supports their efforts. The type A parent's tendency to criticize rather than show support for what goes well for the child also contributes to an environment that does not feel safe for trying new things. The type A person's difficulty with expressing affection or support for others in general has a profoundly limiting effect on how free the child feels to pursue natural growth.

Second, the need for the type A person to control and dominate her or his environment places a tremendously limiting structure around the child's attempts to grow. Imagine a palm tree growing in a terrarium, trying to reach its full potential! It can't be done. As the type A parents push their child into the activities they wish the child to pursue, put down the child's ideas and efforts as a means of staying "superior," use power-oriented styles of discipline, and dominate the running and structure of the home's life-style, the child's natural abilities have little opportunity to emerge. The parents might end up with a nice little showcase child, with whom they can attempt to impress those around them, but the child's personal growth would become stunted by the restriction of that showcase's shell.

While such children do not usually recognize the exact process by which they are being deprived, they can sense that something is missing, something they know they need but are not getting. Because they cannot identify what they lack, their building resentment does not have an appropriate object to which it can attach itself. Thus the child enters adulthood with a sense of free-floating hostility, an ongoing state of anger that cannot be relieved because the offending object—the "non-average" expectable environment—was a variable childhood, which, of course, no longer exists. The type A person's constant seeking of approval and external validation of worth can in itself be seen as a quest for finding that average expectable environment that he or she missed as a child. It is as if the person has become trapped in a stage of development that cannot be completed, since the unconditional positive regard, affection, and supportiveness found by a child in his or her parents is not a relationship that is usually found in adult living. So anger bursts forth any time the adult world does not provide support for the type A person's striving, as it is a reliving of the sense of stifling control he or she perceived as a child.

Again, the sense of anger from having been environmentally stifled need not be a result of type A parenting. All of the traumatic childhood circumstances that promote low self-esteem can also produce this form of anger. The loss of a parent, an abusive childhood situation, poverty, or illness during childhood all can contribute to an environment that leaves a child with a subconscious feeling of resentment over what was not, and never can be, since childhood will never occur again.

Likewise, some of us seem to be born with a tendency toward pessimism or aggressive attitudes. Many parents might discover this in the very beginning, as they compare their children and discover that one of their babies seems so much crabbier than the others. Such a child may turn out to be more difficult to socialize than the others, but it is not a lost cause. Again, we can be born with a tendency to feel a certain way, but how we deal with it is entirely up to us.

LEARNING TYPE A BEHAVIOR

When children experience low self-esteem or status insecurity, they find ways to cope with it. One way children often cope is to rebel against the standards of society. The child perceives himself or herself as having been placed at the bottom of these standards, and learns to protect his or her feelings of worth by denying that the standards matter. The child then engages in all sorts of antisocial behavior because he or she is disregarding those standards. This results in society's labeling the child as "bad" and giving further feedback to the child that he or she is of low value, resulting in more denial and rebellion, and the cycle continues.

Another way children sometimes cope with low self-esteem is to accept it as a reality. The child decides to believe the world's message that he or she is of little value and becomes withdrawn and depressed. The child offers little interaction in the classroom or social settings and often vegetates at home, because the child believes that nothing he or she has to say is of any value, and will probably just end up being criticized or ridiculed anyway. Since the child communicates so little, he or she never gets the feedback from the rest of the world that would point out the child's strengths and positive attributes. The lack of positive feedback is interpreted by the child as being even more evidence that he or she does not measure up, resulting in more depression and withdrawal, and the cycle continues.

Type A behavior and beliefs are yet another avenue through which a child might cope with low self-esteem and status insecurity. It is a way of interacting with the world that provides a balm against looking at feelings of low inner worth. Instead of focusing inwardly toward inherent self-value, the child learns to look outward toward his or her achievements and accomplishments as a measure of worth. As a result, the child turns to overachieving and competition as a way to seek personal value. Since achieving behavior is rewarded by our society, the child is reinforced for his or her protective efforts. However, the child then feels compelled to keep up the same or even higher levels of achievement, for fear that others will discover how "worthless" he or she really is.

Children can learn to defend themselves against low self-worth with type A beliefs and behaviors through interactions with their parents. One of the most significant ways children learn this pattern is by watching the behavior of their parents. Many researchers believe that the majority of children's learning occurs through the effects of modeling by parents and other significant persons. After observing behaviors, children try them out. If the practiced behaviors meet the child's desired ends or are in some other way rewarding, the child will continue to practice them. If the behavior does not get the child what he or she wants or is in some other way punishing, the new behavior is tossed into the discard pile.

Type A parents, of course, model type A behavior. They provide florid examples of overvaluing achievement by placing such a high priority on it in their daily living. How competitiveness is handled is also modeled: You belittle those who lose; you become hostile when you are the loser; and you sacrifice your interpersonal relationships by treating others poorly for the purpose of coming out on top. Concerning competition, type A parents model above all else the attitude that winning is the biggest priority.

How to handle anger, especially the child's swelling sense of free-floating hostility, is also modeled by the type A parent. Children see their type A parents blow up not only when their goals are blocked, but also at any time or in any situation where an outlet can be found. Children watch anger being used as a way to try to dominate others and feel in control. Again, they see a model of sacrificing interpersonal relationships for selfish purposes; specifically, expressing anger in an insensitive and manipulative manner.

These children see how their type A parents scan the world and others for only those aspects that are not perfect, and watch them make sure that their criticisms are known. Thus children learn the behaviors necessary to pacify their own self-esteem by putting down others and manufacturing artificial superiority. The child sees a model of controlling others as a means of defending against insecurity, since the typical type A parent relies so much on overcontrolling within the family system.

Type A parents also model their life-style of back-to-back activity and the priority of staying busy, not "wasting" a second, thereby accomplishing as much as possible within the least amount of time. In this manner, children can learn the mechanics behind living a life filled with hurry sickness and time urgency.

A second contribution type A parents provide to teaching type A behavior is how they may reward it. One of the few things guaranteed to get some form of positive response from a type A parent is a major achievement. The reward value of such a response teaches children that approval and attention are available if they achieve. So these children continue to pursue achievement in the hope of continuing to receive the rewards of approval and attention.

The paradox, however, is that if these children succeed too much, the type A parent begins to feel inadequate in comparison. So the parent begins to point out how the children's accomplishments might be improved upon. Such criticism serves the purpose of allowing the parent to still feel superior, no matter how much the child succeeds. But it also gives the children the message that they must try harder and achieve even more if they are ever to win unconditional parental approval. Thus the child is taught the no-win philosophy that the key to being acceptable is to achieve, but that the child can never achieve enough to be acceptable.

Another behavior that can have reward value for the child involves type A "trashing" behavior. Since the type A person is always on the lookout for something to criticize, such parents can easily empathize with any criticisms of the world that their child might produce. This empathy can be interpreted by the child as a form of approval. It essentially says that trashing behavior is worthy of attention. The child feels rewarded by such attention as well as by the outlet that criticizing provides for the child's own free-floating hostility. The child is likely to continue to search for imperfections to criticize just to feel the reward of being joined in spirit with the parent. There is a power to be felt in this joining, since the parent is seen as the holder of truth and validator of worth, so additional reward value is sensed. And if the parent is joined with the child in criticizing outside variables, at least then the parent won't be criticizing the child, which gives trashing behavior a negative reinforcement value as well.

A third manner in which parents teach type A behavior involves the family enmeshment process I mentioned earlier. Type A parents are excessively controlling of their child's activities because they experience their child's accomplishments as yet one more barometer of their own self-worth. In this manner, family life can become a miniature "boot camp" for the type A life-style. The parents push their child into multiple activities—often ones that the parents themselves had always wanted to succeed at—and devote tremendous enthusiasm and domineering techniques toward getting the child to perform well at them. This aspect of type A parenting may be the most active, direct influence toward future type A behavior in a child's life.

In summary, parents teach children type A behavior through modeling, reward systems, and active training. If parenting influences alone were the driving force behind type A behavior, however, we might expect to see a good deal of the effects on children disappear once they left home. Behavior modification theories generally agree that rewarded behaviors continue and punished behaviors cease only for as long as the rewards and punishments are occurring. Once they are taken away, the change in behaviors tend to become extinguished. So we would expect that type A functioning would bite the dust once the child leaves home.

Unfortunately, many mechanisms help maintain type A behavior. Part of its maintenance comes from inside the person, as he or she pampers low self-esteem with the brief feelings of adequacy to be found within the completion of an accomplishment. And since we generally learn to develop relationships with people whose beliefs are similar to ours, these individuals may search for a support system that will help reinforce the ones they learned as children.

But a major source of learning and maintaining type A behavior is our culture itself. Western culture rewards the high achiever. Those who can effectively formulate their personal goals and persistently work toward achieving them can reap our society's fruits of status and material goods. Even a person who is simply gifted with high levels of intelligence and creativity can easily be drawn into this achievement track, as the person is rewarded for just doing what comes naturally. Imagine the increased reward value experienced by the type A person, who not only finds acceptance of his or her achievement orientation and enjoys the rewards our society provides for it, but also finds a new external measure of self-worth that replaces the importance the type A person placed on the opinion of his or her parents. The quest for approval and belief in externally measured worth thus continues in the child as he or she emancipates from the type A home. The difference in the child's functioning is that he or she continues to be shaped by the achievement aspects of our culture—the new object from which to extract personal validation—rather than by the child's parents. In fact, our culture can encourage unhealthy achieving in any child from any family, no matter how the low self-worth and free-floating hostility may have come about. The effects of our culture on type A behavior will be discussed in more depth in a later chapter.

Chapter Four

Becoming a Healthy Achiever

So far, I have been describing mainly unhealthy achieving and how it can develop. For some of us, unhealthy achieving may be the only style of achievement we know. What is a "healthy" achiever? What are the attributes of such a person? Exactly what is it we want to encourage in our children so that their achievement style will be more personally rewarding and less self-destructive?

Shirley Gould has addressed these questions in a book that in some ways was ahead of its time.[1] *The Challenge of Achievement* was published in 1978, a time when type A behavior was only beginning to be defined and treated. Yet, she was able to propose teaching achievement attitudes in ways that are the antithesis of what has only recently been established as lying beneath the functioning of type A families. My framework for healthy achieving is essentially an expansion of observations she has already made, reworked to be applied as an alternative to the type A style of striving.

ATTRIBUTES OF HEALTHY ACHIEVERS

The healthy achiever is self-confident, has self-respect, and has good self-esteem. Because of self-confidence, healthy achievers feel the inner assurance that they can succeed. They believe in themselves and trust in their abilities. Due to self-respect, healthy achievers will not push themselves beyond their abilities, and will invest in the protection of their health and well-being with the same degree of energy and perseverance with which they pursue achievement. And the good self-esteem of healthy achievers is not based on the external appearances of excellence. Instead, healthy achievers learn to accept themselves for who they are, rather than for what they do, who they know, how they look, or what they own.

The healthy achiever is independent and self-sufficient. The independence of healthy achievers is founded on a personal recognition of themselves as autonomously functioning human beings. They recognize and accept their personal responsibility for the consequences of their actions as well as for their lives in general. They can experience and exult in the joy of success just for the joy of exultation, since they are not encumbered by an achieving style that depends on comparisons with others and opinions of others for its direction and intensity. The self-sufficiency of healthy achievers includes recognition of their own limitations, but having the confidence that whatever they cannot provide for themselves can be effectively requested from others in a caring, fair, reciprocal manner. In this way, healthy achievers can seek out what they need to be able to achieve, either from their own or from others' resources, and still remain successful in their interpersonal relationships.

The healthy achiever is comfortable with making decisions. Healthy achievers strive to develop the skills necessary to explore relevant variables and to make intelligent decisions. Likewise, their self-confidence and good self-esteem allow them to risk making decisions involving the possibility of error or failure, since unsuccessful ventures do not catastrophically affect their self-esteem. Thus they feel free to try new things and to work toward new goals, as they rely on their decision-making ability and feel comfortable accepting the consequences for whatever avenues they choose to pursue.

The healthy achiever sees learning as a lifelong venture. Healthy achievers recognize that we never stop developing skills, attaining new knowledge, or growing emotionally and interpersonally. They do not operate with the expectation of being able to say, "By Jove, I think I've made it," because they know that perfection is never reached. Instead, they appreciate learning as being one more experience to be enjoyed in the process of "being." And, in the process of living out this healthy stance toward learning, new goals are reached as a consequence of just contentedly being, rather than as a consequence of frantic striving.

The healthy achiever never feels that it's too late. Healthy achievers live neither in the past nor in the future. They learn from their past and plan in ways that respect the future, but do not let these unduly restrict their present choices. They can make new career moves and expand their interpersonal relationships because they are not emotionally bound up by regrets over their past and anxiety over what might happen in their future.

The healthy achiever is open to change. Healthy achievers base their security on an acceptance of themselves—perhaps including their beliefs, their perceived personality characteristics, and their value system—rather than the external constructs they may find surrounding them. They, therefore, do not feel unrealistically threatened by the changes that may take place in their external world should they pursue something new. Even internal changes, such as adopting a new attitude and examining one's values, are processes they can willingly face, since their inner security flows from self-acceptance rather than from some rigidly defined inner structure. Thus they can change their dysfunctional beliefs and styles of inter-action when they discover that such things are interfering with their ability to achieve.

The healthy achiever is a realistic optimist. While healthy achievers recognize that others have faults, they generally give others the benefit of the doubt. In the same way that they have learned to accept themselves as growing, changing, valuable human beings, they also accept and value others as they act out their own growth experiences. They expect others to err but can care about them and assist them anyway, since they are aware that they err themselves and will place no greater expectations on others than they do on themselves. Such an accepting attitude results in successful interpersonal relationships, an asset not only to the healthy achiever's pursuits, but also to the pursuits of those who know him or her.

Last, and perhaps most important, *the healthy achiever lives a balanced life-style.* Having a balanced life-style is reflected by Shirley Gould as she describes the healthy achiever as being "a cooperating, loving human being who contributes to the well-being of other people as well as himself or herself, in true social interest."[2] The elements balanced by a healthy achiever are personal achievement, interpersonal relationships, the ability to play, and caring about one's fellow human beings. Personal achievement means more than the status-oriented successes typically sanctioned by our society. Instead, personal achievement means feeling contented with one's efforts—not only materialistically or in the work force, but in relating to others as well—and remaining satisfied even if one's efforts are not outwardly successful. Interpersonal relationships are valued by the healthy achiever as highly as his or her achievement efforts. Thus the healthy achiever does not sacrifice relationships for the purpose of achievement. Play and recreation are important to healthy achievers because they provide opportunities for experiencing a nonpressured state of being—with themselves, with others, or even just feeling oneness with nature. It is a time for doing just for the enjoyment of doing. Play provides a time to relax and recollect oneself and to put life in perspective as well as a time for refueling for the work-related aspects of life. Tempering the entire balancing act is an underlying caring about others, a desire to give to others, as well as to join with them, in a mode of seeking community with our fellow human beings.

These attributes differ markedly from what we see in the type A achiever. Within the above framework for healthy achieving, it would be difficult for a person to function simultaneously as a type A achiever and a healthy achiever.

HOW TYPE A ACHIEVER ATTRIBUTES DIFFER

The type A achiever lacks self-confidence and self-respect and lives out a maladaptive philosophy of self-esteem. Type A achievers never reach the unrealistically high levels of success they demand of themselves to be able to experience confidence in their ability to achieve. They never quite trust that they have the ability to accomplish anything, and they must constantly try to prove it to themselves with continual attempts to excel. The type A person's lack of self-respect is evident, as such individuals sacrifice their physical, emotional, and interpersonal well-being to the god of overachieving. And their self-esteem, as I explained in detail earlier, is not based on self-acceptance. Instead, it is wrapped up in an artificial world of appearances.

The type A achiever is neither independent nor self-sufficient. Type A individuals cannot feel good about themselves without receiving or somehow experiencing constant strokes or approval from others. They cannot direct their achievement efforts toward what is personally satisfying because they are too caught up in finding pursuits that will make them look superior or will in some other way impress others. Thus they ultimately depend on others for their direction and for their feelings of sufficiency.

The type A achiever can feel paralyzed by the need to make a decision. The risk type A individuals fear is that they might err, and failure is experienced as a direct attack on their self-esteem. The fear of failure, therefore, clouds issues and may even directly sabotage the effectiveness of the type A person's judgment. The type A person may never feel comfortable deciding to try something new because he or she will most likely not be able to excel at it immediately. This restricts opportunities for new experiences and achievement.

The type A achiever has difficulty with the concept that he or she may have something left to learn. Type A achievers must look flawless—always "right," always "better" than others—in order to feel adequate. Admitting gaps in their knowledge would be an affront to their superiority. The need to protect this image interferes with their ability to put themselves in situations where they play the role of being learners. This can result in their rarely becoming involved in the process of pursuing new experiences or enjoying learning and growth.

The type A achiever bases daily living on events in the past and future. Type A striving is directed by deficits experienced in the past, which supposedly will be made up for by goals they will meet in the future. We live only in the present, and type A individuals may never arrive at the point where they can say, "Right now, this is what I think I would enjoy doing." In this manner they never get around to pursuing what they can truly enjoy.

The type A achiever feels threatened by change other than change that puts him or her in a more superior light. With any life-style change there is a risk that one of the type A achiever's external measures of self-esteem may evaporate. Type A individuals have difficulty changing their inner belief systems as well, since they use their dysfunctional beliefs as a means of fueling behavior directed toward their external appearance of superiority.

The type A achiever is in many ways an "unrealistic pessimist." Type A individuals expect the worst of others and guard against being taken advantage of by others through overcontrolling the environment and finding various ways to bully others into submission. They may manage to establish their "superiority" in this way, but destroy any possibility of closeness with family or coworkers. Being alienated from others eliminates much of the community-related resources they might want to access as they pursue their goals, as well as any chance that they will receive the emotional support we all need from time to time.

And, of course, the type A achiever does not live a balanced life-style. Status-oriented achievement receives the lion's share of the type A achiever's life efforts. The noncompetitive aspects of play, pursuing interpersonal relationships, and expanding social interest fall to the wayside as they narrow their focus onto the road of achievement.

So, as we can see, it would be difficult for a person to be both type A and a healthy achiever. The two personality styles function in almost opposite ways while in the pursuit of achievement. These differing styles reflect the manifestation of differing beliefs, attitudes, and general life philosophies. Next, I will describe these opposing styles in terms of attitudes toward others, toward oneself, and toward the world.

THE PHILOSOPHY OF THE HEALTHY ACHIEVER

The healthy achiever's philosophy toward others is that *all human beings are highly valuable.* This worth is inherent and need not be earned. Healthy achievers have a sense of empathy that is well-developed enough for them to recognize and understand the feelings of others. Their capacity for empathy feeds their caring about others and creates a desire to contribute toward others' well-being. Healthy achievers also value others because the sense of community they experience while engaged with them feels so rewarding. Healthy achievers appreciate others because they recognize the connection we all share just from being human beings.

The healthy achiever's attitude toward the self is one of *self-acceptance.* Healthy achievers do not get caught up in the concept of "self-esteem," which is the idea that you can place a specific value of "good" or "bad" on yourself on the basis of your behavior or attributes. They endeavor to do their best—not for the purpose of self-esteem, but instead for the joy of "doing" and being able to see a job done well. They feel whole and acceptable no matter how their endeavors turn out, even though they recognize their own imperfections and failures.

For the healthy achiever, *the world is an exciting, inviting medium within which to live.* It is here to be explored, shared, and enjoyed. Healthy achievers experience the world as neither unrealistically threatening nor existing solely for narcissistic gain. The world simply is, with both its pleasures and hardships.

THE PHILOSOPHY OF THE TYPE A ACHIEVER

The type A achiever believes that *others are competition*. Others are viewed as either obstacles blocking the road toward achievement or as entities to be used along the way. The type A achiever can have the capacity for empathy, but it may have little opportunity to emerge, since it is overshadowed by the type A achiever's fears of looking inferior or being taken advantage of. Without a well-functioning sense of empathy, it is difficult to enjoy the connectedness to be found with others or to have concern for their well-being. Thus the type A person's beliefs about others are that they are isolating, looking out for their own interests, and certainly not interested in the well-being of the type A person.

The type A achiever's beliefs about the self are clear: *You are your behavior, you are your achievements, and you are what you appear to be to others.* Worth is earned, not innate. The type A person believes that he or she must be perfect, or at least the very best, to be acceptable, and designs his or her life around that belief.

Type A achievers may feel paralyzed by even thinking about their philosophy of the world. The world is seen as immense, disorganized, and hard to control. Their bottom line is that *the world is threatening* and is more of a battleground than a source of enjoyment. It is much easier for the type A person to focus on the little nuts and bolts of what affects him or her personally, rather than on a view of the world, since little things are easier to tamper with. As type A achievers cram their lives with such activity, they can avoid stopping and evaluating their world, as well as any philosophy concerning the meaning of life in general.

The philosophies held by healthy achievers and type A achievers play a major role in the way they eventually run their lives. Next, we will look at how such philosophies interplay with our feelings and behaviors.

HOW OUR PHILOSOPHIES AFFECT OUR BEHAVIOR

Most people don't think about how their beliefs and attitudes may be connected to their feelings or choices of behavior. On the surface, feelings appear to be controlled by the environment. After all, when someone performs a kindness for us, we feel happy. If it rains on a day when we planned to go on a picnic, we feel disappointed. When mail-order companies mess up or lose our orders, we feel irritated. If somebody takes advantage of us or acts cruelly toward us, we feel angry.

The truth of the matter is that our feelings are not caused by situations or by other people. Instead, the way we think about a situation or another person's actions leads us to feel a certain way.

For example, imagine that you are walking along a crowded city sidewalk when, suddenly, someone comes up from behind and knocks you over. Most likely, as you are sitting on the ground, perhaps feeling a little bruised and startled, you would also start feeling a little angry, right? Then suppose as you begin to get up, you discover that you are looking into the face of a panting German shepherd wearing a sign that reads, "Don't pet me, I'm working" and that the dog is being closely followed by a woman wearing dark glasses. Would you still feel so angry? Probably not. You might still feel somewhat irritated and embarrassed over the indignity of being knocked flat in front of a crowd of people, but you would not be nearly so angry as you would have become had your fall been caused by someone's being careless, insensitive, or purposely abusive.

You see, between the occurrence of any event and the experiencing of a subsequent feeling, we consciously or subconsciously evaluate what has happened. This evaluation, and not the actual event, determines how we will feel. In the preceding illustration, your thoughts at first might have gone something like this: "How dare that person push me over! She had no right to do that. She should have watched where she was going!" Such thoughts produce the feeling of anger. After seeing that you had been run into by a blind person, your conscious or subconscious thoughts might have gone more like this: "Oh, it was an accident. She meant me no harm." These sorts of thoughts do not promote anger, and in fact might induce feelings of compassion and concern for the blind woman. So if feelings were truly caused by outer circumstances alone, you would not have the differing feelings illustrated by these two evaluative processes.

Feelings in turn affect our choices of behavior. When we feel hurt by the way someone has treated us, we might choose to withdraw. If we feel attacked or threatened by another, we might choose to become defensive. If we are touched by another in a way that feels loving, we might choose to express love in return.

Continuing with the earlier example, imagine what your choices of behavior might have been for the two possible scenarios. If you had become angry, you would most likely be choosing from a pool of behaviors, including telling the woman off, giving her an icy glare, letting loose a string of profanities, or physically retaliating. If you had felt compassion and concern for the blind woman, you would instead be more focused on getting up and making sure she hadn't become disoriented because of the stumble and needed some form of assistance.

Therefore, our thoughts have the greatest impact on how we eventually choose to react to what goes on around us. And our thoughts are closely tied to our personal philosophies about the world, about others, and about ourselves. Let's look at how the philosophies of the healthy achiever and the type A achiever would be likely to affect them in a challenging situation. Imagine the following scenario.

A secretary, whom I will call Katie, is working in a busy office and has just completed a major typing job for one of her superiors. A number of other assignments were put on hold as she was focusing on completing this project, since it was a crucial document for an important meeting the following morning. She turns in the project and dives into the various tasks that had been neglected. An hour later, as her superior returns with the document, she immediately notices that he has liberally scribbled over and changed various portions. Apparently he had forgotten some important element, and the changes were truly necessary. Unfortunately, this means that the document will need to be retyped, and Katie will need to put in overtime to do so. This is a tremendous inconvenience to her, since she had plans for that evening.

First, let's look at how the unhealthy achiever's philosophies about others, self, and the world might dictate how Katie might think, feel, and react in this situation.

Others: *Others are competition and look out only for their own interests.*

Thoughts:
* "That insensitive boob!"
* "How could he be so inconsiderate? If he was interested in anybody's needs besides his own, he would have used a little more foresight."
* "I don't like being used and taken advantage of!"
* "It's not fair that I should pay for his mistakes."

Feelings concerning others:
* Anger
* Frustration
* A desire to retaliate

Choices of behaviors she might consider:
* Tell him off
* Fume quietly
* Take her time getting the project done
* Hit him
* Tell everybody else in the office what a jerk he is

* Tell him she's quitting and that he can find someone else to type his stupid report

The Self: *You are your behavior, achievements, and what you appear to be to others.*

Thoughts:
* "I should have gone over it with him before typing it. Boy, am I a failure."
* "If I were more competent I'd be able to do all of these things without falling behind."
* "If I don't get this done, everyone will think it's all my fault, and nobody will think well of me anymore."

Feelings concerning herself:
* Depression
* Low self-worth
* Pressured to prove herself
* Anxiety over whether she can finish her work

Choices of behavior she might consider:
* Become quiet and socially withdrawn, so as not to draw attention to her inadequacy
* Work like crazy to get caught up in everything, to the point of neglecting her health and social activity
* Give up on being able to succeed and plod along so slowly that various tasks don't get done on time, eventually leading to her demotion.

The World: *The world is threatening.*

Thoughts:
* "There's no way I can be successful at this, the way fate works out."
* "Life sure would be easier if the world wasn't out to screw me over."
* "No matter how hard I try, I have no control over my destiny."
* "Life's a bitch and then you die."

Feelings concerning the world:
* Despair
* Helplessness
* Overwhelmed
* The need to self-protect or become defensive

Choices of behavior she might consider:
* Look for a less challenging job
* Gripe at everybody, as she tries to keep up with the apparent dictates of her job
* Push herself toward looking superior in some other life pursuit
* Build "walls" between herself and co-workers, and avoid feeling enjoyment on the job so she can't be let down by her world
* Look for ways of getting some control, like bullying or manipulating those around her into gratifying her needs

Clearly, if Katie holds the type A philosophies of others, of herself, and of the world, she is likely to be tempted to engage in some behaviors that are hurtful, maladaptive, and ultimately self-destructive. By contrast, let's look at how the healthy achiever's philosophies about others, about the self, and about the world would play themselves out through Katie's thoughts, feelings, and potential choices of behavior during the same situation.

Others: *All human beings are highly valuable.*

Thoughts:
* "This is an inconvenience, but I'm sure he didn't do this on purpose."
* "I imagine he feels bad that he put me in this position."
* "He must feel quite anxious over whether or not I can get this done in time for the meeting."

Feelings concerning others:
* Irritated over the inconvenience, but having a sense of conciliated understanding of its necessity
* Disappointed that she will probably have to change her plans for the evening, but knowing that she will have other opportunities for socializing
* Concern over the feelings of her supervisor
* Concern over whether the project will get done on time for him

Choices of behavior she might consider:
* Inform her supervisor of her situation and point out its inconvenience, but that she will make every effort to see to it that the project gets done

* See if she can enlist the help of one of the other secretaries
* Contact her friends and arrange to go out later in the evening or on another day
* Reassure her superior that she doesn't hold the error against him; after all, she makes mistakes too
* Offer to help him with organizing and editing future major projects before they are in the final stages

The Self: *I am acceptable.*

Thoughts:
* "It would be nice if I could juggle virtually any amount of work tossed before me, but that would be an unrealistic expectation of myself. Nobody could do that."
* "Others might be upset with me if I don't get everything done, and that's unfortunate. But I will still feel good about myself and my efforts, since I try my best to get things done."

Feelings concerning herself:
* Curious to see how well she will pull this one off
* Confident that she will put in her best effort
* Excited about the possibility of personal growth occurring as a result of the experience

Choices of behavior she might consider:
* Organize and prioritize what needs to be done
* Enlist the advice and assistance of others as needed
* Put out her best effort to complete her work

The World: *The world is an exciting, inviting medium within which to live.*

Thoughts:
* "I wonder how I might best use resources to organize this."
* "Here we go; another new adventure!"
* "What things might I be able to do or suggest that would result in less of this sort of thing happening to me as well as to others?"

Feelings about the world:
* Challenged by the mission before her
* Eager to see what she will learn or what new coping strategies she might develop from this experience she has encountered
* A desire to contribute in some way that will help make the world more easily accessible for meeting people's needs

Choices of behavior she might consider:
* Look for the most efficient way to use available environmental resources
* Work hard as a means of learning from this experiential "gift"
* Talk to her superiors about the possibility of getting a word processor, so last minute retypes will not be so time consuming
* Talk to her superiors about developing some sort of policy concerning last minute overtime so that secretaries are not unreasonably inconvenienced

In summary, the healthy achiever's philosophies about others, about the self, and about the world result in thoughts, feelings, and behavioral impulses that are positive, constructive, and aimed toward growth and healthy achieving. By contrast, the type A achiever's philosophies direct a person toward pessimism, maladaptive behavior, and ultimate self-destruction.

As the situation eventually played itself out, either philosophy could result in the same course of action being taken. As either a healthy achiever or a type A achiever, Katie might decide to bite the bullet and work like crazy. But the differences between her emotional reactions to the situation would be substantial. While as a healthy achiever she would be focusing on the process of accomplishment and feeling challenged and excited, as a type A achiever she would be focusing on the threat of failure and having been wronged by others, and would feel anxious, angry, or even depressed. After completion of the task either way, she might feel exhausted at the end of the day. But as a healthy achiever, the fatigue would be the type felt when one puts in a good day's efforts, while as a type A achiever she would be experiencing the backlash from reacting to excess norepinephrine and feeling emotionally drained.

Friedman and Ulmer have worked for many years with type A cardiovascular patients and their maladaptive attitudes and behaviors.[3] Their patients discovered that in spite of the fact that they had changed their worldview, they were still getting as much done as they were before, if not more. We do not need anger, pessimism, or fear of the threat of failure to drive us toward our accomplishments. Achievement can flow just as well, if not more easily, from simply learning to enjoy the process of doing and being in our world.

When I was in junior high school we had a teacher who had a reputation for being a little eccentric. He had some odd mannerisms and set ways of looking at the world that many of us found to be quite comical. But he had one pet phrase that has stuck with me to this very day. Whenever he found himself in a position of having to confront students about their behavior, he would remind them, "It is *strictly* a question of your attitude." We would often mimic the manner in which he would say this, speaking with clipped, overly polished syllables and putting special emphasis on rolling an extended "r" in the word *strictly*. Few of us took him seriously at the time. Yet, the kernel of truth he was attempting to pass on was not far from the concept I have been describing throughout this chapter. The attitude we have toward ourselves, others, and the world and what achievement means to us personally can make all the difference in how we choose to run our lives.

How do we teach our children to have a healthy attitude toward achievement? This can be especially difficult if we haven't adopted it ourselves. The answer to this question comes in two parts: (1) training children in specific ways that encourage healthy achieving and (2) becoming aware of our own behavioral tendencies and how we might inadvertently pass on unhealthy achievement philosophies to our children. The next two chapters will address each of these aspects of childrearing.

Not too long ago a friend of mine shared with me a story from his childhood.[4] When he was young, he and a friend of his would often go to the zoo together. One of their favorite activities was to harass a troop of fiercely competitive monkeys that happened to be housed there. The boys had found that if they threw something into the cage, the monkeys would put on quite a show as they all attempted to take ownership of the new object. They were not particularly discriminating. No matter what the boys threw in, the monkeys would all scream and push and claw and fight until one monkey finally emerged from the crowd as the victor. The troop would then settle down until the next "prize" was tossed into the ring, and round two of the performance would begin.

One day as the boys were scrounging through the zoo garbage cans in search of new bait, they found that someone had thrown out a substantial amount of pink cotton candy. The monkeys had never seen anything like this before. Each time the boys threw in a wad, the monkeys would really go wild, especially after they found out it was edible. However, this particular troop of monkeys also had a habit of washing everything before eating it. So as the champ would emerge, waving the cotton candy above his head as if it were an Olympic gold medal, he would immediately scramble over to the water trough and rinse it off. Of course, as the monkey would raise his hands out of the water, he would find that his prize had vanished.

We often find that we are behaving the same as these monkeys—screaming and pushing and clawing and fighting our way toward some all-important goal—only to find that once we attain it, its importance dissolves before our eyes.

This particular friend and I had just finished graduate programs when we had this discussion. We noted how we had put "living" aside for literally years in order to reach the all-important goal of getting a degree and how we had planned on rejoining the world of the living once we were finished. But what we found as we left school was not what we had expected.

First of all, we discovered that the hoops to be jumped through did not end at commencement. There were licensing exams, getting established in a position, as well as other professional mountains that needed to be scaled—and could just as easily become the new future goals that must be reached before living could begin.

Second, we came to recognize that during our schooling we had gotten to know some pretty nice people. In fact, our degree programs had been so intense that we had banded together with our fellow students as a means of surviving, and thus developed some unique and very close relationships with our fellow sojourners. Yet, at the end of all our *sturm und drang*, when we had reached the goals that we thought would mark the beginning of life, we realized that reaching the goals meant bringing an end to the relationships that had kept us living, as our colleagues all took off for various positions around the globe.

"I see it like this," my friend told me. "We have been chasing a rainbow all this time in hope of finding the pot of gold at the rainbow's end. We've found the pot, but we've discovered that the pot is empty. The gold was scattered along the way; we just never stopped to pick it up."

Since we had chosen to direct our lives around some future event, we missed out on the true gold to be found in the here and now. Some of the dearest and most intimate relationships we have had in our lives, and maybe ever will, have now ended, never to exist in the same way again. I suppose we'll stay in touch over the years and will maintain relationships of some sort. Likewise, we will form new friendships as we move on, friendships that may even be as satisfying as the ones we had during our training. But they will never be the same as those we once had, but did not take the time to fully appreciate and enjoy. In a seeming blink of an eye, that moment has passed.

Grieving will not bring back the lost moments of life. And spending all of one's time mourning the past is just as dysfunctional as focusing only on future goals. But being aware that the loss has occurred allows us to learn and to appreciate better what we have in the present. I can see now that during my daily living there will always be a file to complete, a phone call to make, a chapter to write, cookies to bake, and a floor to vacuum. I know now that all of these can wait long enough for me to stop and enjoy the "gold" that makes life livable. It is this philosophy—appreciating oneself, others, the world, and time itself—that saves us from losing our lives in the sea of our achievements.

Chapter Five

Healing the Parent

Children are quick to recognize hypocrisy. We cannot expect them to steer away from type A behavior just because we tell them to, when they see their parents modeling type A behavior right and left. Thus an important component to encouraging our children to become healthy achievers is to get a handle on our own unhealthy achieving style.

This chapter briefly describes how type A individuals might go about healing emotionally, interpersonally, physically, and spiritually. It is by no means intended as a complete treatment program for type A behavior, post-myocardial infarction patients, and the like, although it could be used as an aid to such a treatment program. Instead, this chapter gives you a chance to begin doing something about difficulties you may have recognized in yourself in earlier chapters. If you suffer from only a few fleeting symptoms, the guidance given within this chapter may be all you need to get your type A behavior under control. If your symptoms are severe, you may want the assistance of a therapist to work through the underpinnings of your type A behavior.

HEALING EMOTIONALLY

The last chapter showed how our philosophies dictate our thoughts, how our thoughts lead to our feelings, and how our feelings influence our choices of behavior. A large portion of healing emotionally involves examining our thought lives. We can't jump in and change only our feelings—unless we're using medications or some other neuropsychological means. Besides, feelings are normal physiological responses, and to try to turn them off at one juncture would only mean having them resurface elsewhere.

Feelings are normal reactions to how we perceive what is going on around us. When we are in a potentially dangerous situation, we feel fear. This fear—plus a few hormonal juices—activates us toward protecting ourselves. Unfortunately, type A individuals react emotionally as if they are in life-threatening situations when in reality the "threats" are either minimal, inconsequential, or nonexistent. Changing how we perceive our situations, or how we evaluate them, calms these overreactions.

The classic type A achiever believes that others look out only for themselves, that the world is threatening, and that a person's worth and identity are based on his or her achievements and appearances. How can such deeply ingrained beliefs possibly be altered? Actually, they can, but it takes practice. These dysfunctional beliefs, when repeatedly challenged, can be replaced with more rational beliefs.

The beliefs that the world and others are threatening are in many ways accurate. There is the threat of nuclear war, the threat of the ozone layer's burning out, the destruction of the ecology, AIDS, the drug world, and so on. However, it is not the end of the world if the car in front of you is moving too slowly, if your boss doesn't like your new idea, or if your spouse wants to watch a different television program from the one you want to watch. Are these trivial situations really worth destroying your cardiovascular system over? Of course not. They have nuisance value, naturally, but feeling a little irritated is vastly more healthy than being so angry that you send your blood pressure sky high.

It could be that the irrationality of some of your destructive thoughts is already obvious to you, but that you are having difficulty putting your "catastrophizing" to rest. You find yourself repeatedly playing some old mental tape from a past hurt, which results in your continuously overreacting. "You never get anything right"; "What a dumb idea"; "How could anyone love a loser like you?"; "The sky will fall if I don't get control of this"; or some other tape might cloud over your efforts to tell yourself, "Hey, I can handle it."

One excellent way of dealing with this kind of interference is called the "rubber band technique." Wear a rubber band on your wrist at all times. Whenever you find destructive thoughts raging through your consciousness, snap the rubber band on the tender side of your wrist. Most people find this to be painful enough to make adjustments in their thoughts. After about a week or two, many people find that their catastrophizing and obsessing over trivia have decreased to the point where they no longer need to use the rubber band.

Some people have devoted so much of their lives to worrying about potential threats that they have difficulty teaching themselves healthy alternative beliefs. One method for counteracting old beliefs and building healthier ones involves using three-by-five-inch cards. On one side, write down one of your destructive beliefs. On the other side, write down the healthier alternative.

For example, if you often find yourself saying, "If I don't succeed at this, I am a real loser," write this down on one side of the card. On the other side, write down beliefs more consistent with those of healthy achievers, such as, "I am valuable as a person whether I succeed or fail"; "I may not succeed, but I will be sure to learn something"; or "Winning is fun, but I enjoy participating just because I enjoy this activity." Make a different card for every destructive belief that you find to be influencing you. When you find one of the destructive thoughts occurring, whip out the corresponding card, read the belief out loud, then turn the card over and read out loud the healthier belief three times.

Some people find that their destructive thoughts are so deeply ingrained that they no longer are aware of the "thought" part of their behavioral patterns. To them, events lead to feelings, and then to behaviors, or perhaps they see only events leading to their behaviors, without even an awareness of what feelings might be involved. One book that is useful for helping to identify the full pattern is *You Can Change How You Feel* by Gerald Kranzler.[1] If bibliotherapy does not appeal to you, or it does not seem to help you become aware of your corresponding thoughts and feelings, you might find it helpful to seek the aid of a counselor, a psychiatrist, or a psychologist. The most useful therapist for this endeavor would be one with a cognitive-behavioral orientation. Many state psychological associations and community mental-health centers can help you find such a therapist.

In addition to healing their thought-lives as a means of healing emotionally, type A individuals also need to establish a healthier sense of identity. Rather than have their identities wrapped up in what they do, who they know, what they own, and how they look to others, type A individuals need to learn who they are as persons, in the absence of these external indicators of personhood.

Here is one useful exercise for finding the difference between who you are and what you do. Make a list of all of the roles you play in the world: parent, spouse, accountant, secretary, cook, gardener, chauffeur, golfer, bowler, and so on. Be as inclusive as possible. Next, start a second list of everything describing who you are as a person *in the absence of* the roles on the first list. What type of a person are you? What are your likes and dislikes? How would another person describe you? What are your moods like? What personality characteristics would you say you had?

In reality, this second list is who you really are. The first list is just the collection of ways in which you mesh with society. Case in point: Say there is a person who plays the roles of wife, mother, seamstress, volunteer worker, and housekeeper. She is involved in a tragic car accident, in which her family is killed and she is left a quadriplegic. This accident in one fell swoop has wiped out all of the roles she had played in society. Does this mean she is no longer a person? Of course not. However, her second list would remain predominantly the same: the sensitive, caring person; the person who likes ice cream and dislikes disco music; the person who enjoys a good challenge and likes to tell jokes. Her disposition would most likely be altered as a product of the tragedy she had endured, but we all make adjustments in who we are as part of the natural process of change and growth.

There are many women in the world who play the roles of wife, mother, seamstress, volunteer worker, and house-keeper. Does this mean that all of these women are the same person? Obviously not. They are simply all people who play the same collection of roles in our society. Are our roles, then, unimportant, meaningless, and deserving to be devalued? On the contrary, our choices of roles say a lot about who we are as people. We often take pride in our roles as well. But this is different from saying that we *are* what we *do*. My saying "I am a writer" states a particular role I play. My saying "I am a person who enjoys writing" reflects who I am as a person, and I will probably continue to be a person who enjoys writing, whether or not I am currently so employed.

This enlightened sense of identity is useful in helping us identify with healthy achievers' beliefs about themselves, such as "I am a valuable person, whether or not I succeed." A healthy achiever recognizes that achievements are a product of the roles we play. Roles can always be evaluated as successful or unsuccessful, best or worst, or right or wrong. On the contrary, who we are as a person is simply who we are. Our personal preferences, desires, and temperaments cannot be framed in terms of winning or losing; only external behaviors can be evaluated in that way. Thus it is impossible to say that a person is good or bad. A person simply is, and our unique personal characteristics make all of us special, valuable, and of great worth, regardless of what our scorecard looks like in the games of roles, behaviors, and achievements.

HEALING INTERPERSONALLY

How we interact with others is probably the most significant aspect of our type A behavior as we parent. Both free-floating hostility and time urgency encourage behaviors that can squelch a child's sense of self-worth as well as model modes of behavior that we would prefer not be modeled back for us. This section will look at ways we might improve on our interpersonal lives in terms of anger management, assertiveness, and trust.

Anger Management

The anger of a type A individual takes many forms, since the free-floating hostility can latch on to any opportunity for release. One of the most interpersonally damaging times it exposes itself is during blow-ups. So we will begin by looking at various ways of controlling impulsively expressed anger.

One of the most common practices people use while trying to manage their anger is to count to ten. This technique has probably hung around for as long as it has because it, in fact, works. Impulsive anger is experienced on an emotional level, and counting to ten gives the angry person time to put himself or herself back into cognitive control, rather than emotional control. There are other stalling tactics that are also effective. Yelling "Stop!" either in your head or out loud can help break up your immediate reaction. Leaving the room, when possible, also provides a little more space for getting some perspective on the problem and reacting more appropriately.

Diaphragmatic breathing is another stalling tactic, and it also seems to be emotionally calming. In order to breath from the diaphragm, inhale by expanding only the stomach area, not the chest. Breathe in over ten counts, hold in your breath for ten counts, then release it over ten counts. Repeat the process two times.

Once you have your immediate impulsive anger under control, you can begin working on how some of your thought processes are promoting your angry responses. The pattern for anger works the same way it was described earlier for emotional healing: A frustrating or otherwise aversive event occurs, we appraise or evaluate the situation, we react angrily on the basis of this appraisal, and we react behaviorally on the basis of our angry reaction.[2]

The appraisals or evaluations that promote anger usually involve the words *should* or *shouldn't*: "He shouldn't have done that"; "She should have done this"; or even "Life should be fair." More fuel can be added to the fire by such thoughts as "It's awful if I don't get what I deserve" and "I must be treated fairly, or else it is terrible." And eventual aggressive behavior can result when we endorse such thoughts as "I must become upset if things do not go the way I think they should" and "When people upset me I must get back at them."

These thoughts are all irrational. It would be nice if life went the way we thought it should, but nowhere is it written that we are entitled to an easy go of it. The world would be better if everyone treated everybody else fairly, but the complexities of life often make that impossible. It would be preferable if nobody made mistakes and everybody did things perfectly, but unfortunately that is not characteristic of human beings. The "shoulds" and "shouldn'ts" of the world make great goals, but when we start demanding that these goals become the reality that everybody acts out, they then become dysfunctional.

Looking beyond whether anger-promoting beliefs are true or not, we see that these beliefs are irrational just because of what they do to us. Why believe something that makes you miserable, leads you to behave in ways that make others miserable, and damages your cardiovascular system?

Beliefs that promote anger can be disputed in the same way described for other emotional healing. For example, remember Katie the secretary in the last chapter? If she were living by the belief that others only look out for their own interests, her thoughts would promote a significant amount of anger: "That insensitive boob! He deserves to be cut down to size. It's not fair that I should pay for his mistakes."

On the other hand, if she believed that all human beings are highly valuable, she might have given her employer the benefit of the doubt: "This sure is an inconvenience, and he certainly wasn't being very thoughtful, but I don't think he did it on purpose. I don't like having to change my plans because of someone else's mistake, but it's not the end of the world."

Notice that these thoughts still cause some uncomfortable feelings—irritation over the inconvenience and regret over the missed evening of socializing. However, this is drastically different from feeling enraged, vengeful, and ready to lash out. And feeling inconvenienced is much easier to cope with than feeling ready to pop a cork.

Two additional resources that are useful for learning to dispute angry thoughts are David Burns's *Feeling Good* and Albert Ellis's and Robert Harper's *A New Guide to Rational Living*.[3]

Assertiveness

Once the angry cognitions are being managed, the collection of potential behaviors from which to choose changes. Feeling irritated—which one might legitimately feel during a frustrating situation—does not bring to mind the same sorts of behavior as does feeling ready to blow one's stack. So the next step is to build a new style of reacting during frustrating situations.

Type A individuals often get their way with others, but often not as a product of being assertive. During their striving for control, pursuit of getting things exactly right, and being the best, they often leave tread marks over the top of those in their path. An assertive person only asserts his or her rights in ways that do not neglect the rights and feelings of others.[4]

Learning to express anger assertively, rather than aggressively, can mend a mile of fences in a type A individual's interpersonal life. Who wants to spend time around someone who blows up indiscriminately, aggressively takes control of every situation, and expresses cynicism at every turn?

The first lesson in assertiveness is learning to take responsibility for your own feelings. Nobody "makes" you mad; only you and your beliefs can do that. Can people whom you find to be irritating actually reach inside your head and stimulate all the neurons necessary for an angry response to occur? Of course not. Does a frustrating situation send out mysterious vibes that magically stimulate the above said neurons? It is not likely. Again, how we perceive our situation or others is what will determine our emotions, not the situation or other individuals themselves.

Taking responsibility for your feelings involves learning a new vocabulary. Instead of saying, "This screw-up really makes me angry" or "He really ticks me off," assertive expression of anger includes such phraseology as: "I feel angry when you do that"; "You have no right to do this, and I get really irritated when you do it"; and "I get bent out of shape when I have to deal with this sort of thing."

Katie could have expressed her anger aggressively by saying: "You insensitive boob! Do you think the world revolves around you? Find someone else to type your stupid report. And get a life while you're at it!"

Or she could have expressed her anger assertively: "I find this to be a real inconvenience, and I don't appreciate having to change my personal plans because of a problem that I did not cause."

And if last-minute overtime was not a part of her working agreement, she might also have assertively taken a stand: "I realize that you are in a bind, but I already have plans for the evening. One of the other typists here might be interested in overtime pay, and if not, I know of some freelancers who might be interested."

Katie may not have been obligated to bail out her boss by finding another typist, but here is where social interest comes into play. Since she was aware that her employer was distressed and anxious over having the report ready on time, she sympathized with his plight and offered some possible solutions. Afterward she would feel good about herself because she both stood up for her rights and still helped a fellow human being meet his needs. Contrast this with how she might have felt had she just stomped out and lost her job, or worse yet, still had to work around an employer who probably didn't care much for her after experiencing her temper tantrum.

Here are some other hints that can help you react assertively, rather than aggressively:

1. Learn to recognize the types of events, people, and behaviors that seem to be related to your becoming angry. Keep a journal of situations in which you lose your cool, so you can analyze them for patterns of thoughts, feelings, and behaviors.

2. If you know you are about to enter a potentially explosive situation, figure out ahead of time how you might express yourself assertively.

3. Do not sit and stew about things that do not go the way you would prefer. This only leads to an emotional build up that guarantees difficulty in containing your anger the next time you are in a frustrating situation. If you find yourself constantly ruminating your way through frustrating, unfair, and other anger-producing cognitions, try the rubber band technique discussed earlier.

4. Deal with difficulties when they first come up, rather than resentfully going along with them until you become too angry to respond appropriately.

5. Remember that others are entitled to their anger as well as being responsible for it. You do not need to retaliate because others lose their temper, but you can assertively state that you do not appreciate their taking out their anger on you and that you do not see their sarcasm, name-calling, or put-downs as being necessary.

6. Keep in mind that anger and aggression are not the same thing. Anger is an emotion, while aggression is a behavior that can occur with or without the presence of anger. The choice of what you do when you are angry is yours.

For additional help in working on assertive behavior, you might consider reading *Your Perfect Right: A Guide to Assertive Behavior* by Robert Alberti and Michael Emmons.[5]

Trust

The main type A attitude toward others is that of cynicism: that people don't really care about anything besides their own interests; that others are basically frustrating; and that they're probably incompetent as well. Redford Williams discusses this aspect of type A behavior in his book, *The Trusting Heart: Great News About Type A Behavior*.[6] He points out that the ability to learn to trust others, in itself, may reduce the likelihood of responding with type A behavior.

When we do not trust others, we expect the worst of them. Such cynicism shows in our facial expressions, our mannerisms, and how we choose to interact with others. The result is a sort of self-fulfilling prophecy, since people generally do what they perceive as being expected of them. In addition, every little human mistake made by others is often viewed by a type A person as being "proof" that others are incompetent and self-centered, which serves the purpose of reinforcing the cynical attitude.

Redford Williams describes a twelve-step process we can use for developing a more trusting heart: (1) keep track of your cynical thoughts; (2) acknowledge that your cynicism is causing problems for you; (3) use thought-stopping techniques when you find you are having cynical thoughts; (4) after stopping the cynical thinking, focus on less cynical explanations for the situation; (5) think about what the situation was like for the other person; (6) learn to laugh at your suspicious nature; (7) find ways to relax; (8) look for opportunities in your life for demonstrating trust toward others; (9) learn to listen to others, rather than interrupting with your own ideas; (10) practice assertiveness; (11) pretend that each day is your last day on earth; and (12) practice forgiving.[7]

This plan includes many things we have already covered, and it includes this additional special ingredient: the concept of empathy. Develop realistic expectations of others. Recognize that they have feelings the same as you do. How might you be feeling if you were in their place? Does this give you some understanding of why they reacted the way they did? And you would like to be forgiven if you erred. Why not extend this courtesy to others?

Trust is a choice. We can never prove that any individual is completely trustworthy; and due to human error alone, everyone has the potential to let us down at some point. But does this mean that we must treat others as if they can never be trusted? Whom would you rather spend time with, someone who trusts you or someone who is always suspicious of your motives? Would you share your innermost thoughts and feelings with someone who did not trust you? Would you want to marry someone who did not trust you? To what extent do we destroy any chances for intimacy with an inability to trust?

If a person has proven himself or herself to be untrustworthy time and time again, perhaps it is a good idea to be guarded in your relationship with that person. But is it really that the person is always untrustworthy, or is it that you are focusing only on the times the person has failed and ignoring all the times the person has come through for you?

Trust means not only giving people the benefit of the doubt, but also trusting that they are not that different from ourselves. There will always be people whom we cannot reach with our kindness and understanding. But the vast majority are our "soul brothers and sisters," asking the same life questions and living the same life struggles as we do ourselves. The wealth of intimacy and understanding we can reap from our relationships with others is worth the effort of attacking our cynicism. Don't cheat yourself out of receiving this wonderful gift.

HEALING PHYSICALLY

I am not a physician and make no claim to being able to give advice on what is medically appropriate for you. The best person for this sort of advice is your personal physician. However, if you are a full-blown classic type A achiever, it may have been literally decades since you have had a complete physical examination. If this describes you, I fully recommend that you do so.

Assuming that your physician finds you to be a basically healthy person, there are many simple things you can do to improve your physical well-being. In essence, what you need to promote is a more balanced life-style.

Manage your stress. Use the cognitive strategies described earlier to calm yourself during stressful periods. Learn to make use of relaxation techniques (as will be described in the next section concerning spiritual healing). Organize your time more realistically to limit the number of stressors you have to deal with at any one time.

Eat healthily. Limit your intake of caffeine, alcohol, sugar, salt, and fat and increase your intake of high fiber foods, such as fruits, vegetables, and whole grains. **CAUTION:** Do not fall into a type A extremist interpretation of the above, which would be that since we should limit certain foods they are all bad; they're poison and, therefore, should not be consumed at all. Anybody who goes on an eating regimen that allows for no sugar or fat does not stand much chance of sticking to that diet for long. Learn to moderate your eating habits, not torture yourself.

Quit smoking. In addition to what the Surgeon General has to say about smoking, we have learned that it has a behavioral backlash as well. As long as you habitually calm yourself by sticking a cigarette in your mouth, you limit your opportunities for learning more healthy ways to manage your stress or alter your type A response patterns.

Get moderate exercise. Find an activity you enjoy and

pursue it. And don't forget about the Chevy with the cracked rings! You don't need to push yourself to your outer limits to experience the benefits of exercise. Friedman and Ulmer argue that you are actually putting yourself at risk if you do.[8] Seek the advice of trained professionals before you consider any extreme exercise program.

Make time for play and relaxation. Schedule a time every day when you will do something—anything—that comes under the category of "not work." You might take a nap, spend time with your family, read an entertaining book, see a movie—anything that will take you out of the mind-frame of "working." Play is a time to get back in touch with yourself as a person, and it helps you to replenish your energy.

Have a good laugh every day. Laughter really is the best medicine. Humor can be introduced in all aspects of our daily lives. Go for the joke, when the opportunity arises; you can get back to business afterward. Get a joke book, find a sitcom that you like, learn to laugh at yourself during your own human foibles, find the humor in otherwise stressful situations. It doesn't matter whether other persons' humor is different; you are laughing for your own well-being. Let them laugh for theirs.

HEALING SPIRITUALLY

Recently the family of one of our daughter's friends, who is Cambodian, honored us by including us in a Sunday gathering of their people. We drove out into the countryside, where a Buddhist temple was in the process of being constructed. While the men continued in their work on the building, the women were inside, busily preparing a variety of Cambodian delicacies. After the monks had been served, everybody feasted happily, sitting or standing in informal groups and visiting with friends and family. After the meal the children and teenagers performed traditional

Cambodian dances. The dances were neither exhibitionistic nor dazzling. Instead, the dancers gracefully and artistically acted out the simple pleasures of living: the appreciation of a flower or bird; young men and women going down to the river to catch fish—or each other. The atmosphere of the entire gathering was filled with their gentle, quiet spirits. Western culture would not describe this event as being worship. In fact, our new friends called it a *celebration* of Buddha, a joining together in appreciation for all that they had.

Yet, these people had experienced more tragedy and hardship than most of us will ever endure. Some of their children's earliest memories were of running from the Khmer Rouge and being shot at. They had left their families, friends, culture, and homeland to relocate in a foreign country. Scattered over the area, they were reunited as a community only by events like the one we attended.

Most certainly, their experiences of parting from their homeland have left scars. In spite of it all, however, they have managed to maintain their spirits, that essence of being that is life itself. They can appreciate the joy of creation and oneness with others regardless of the pitfalls their daily lives might bring them. The restoration of this spirit can be a powerful tool for the type A achiever as well.

The healing of the spirit—however you might choose to describe that entity—is an amorphous and elusive affair. It is often left for the men and women of religion to define, since scientists feel uncomfortable with defining something so unobservable and unmeasurable. Yet, in the healing of type A attitudes, the calming of the tortured spirit can provide more inner relief that any of the other intervention points.

"Does this mean I have to become a holy roller?" the skeptical type A person might ask. "Is going door-to-door and passing out pamphlets going to cure my heart problem?"

The spirit is especially hard for the type A person to consider changing because it is not external. Type A individuals thrive on finding external activity at which to succeed. Succeeding at inner healing does not have much appeal, since it cannot be directly observed and thus cannot be used to impress others or receive validation of self-worth. And since it can't be directly touched, seen, or heard, it seems even more difficult to try to control. Type A individuals feel much more at home with science, since it deals more with manipulating the variables of the external world.

But science itself is actually as much a faith as a fundamentalist religion. Scientific method is a system of understanding why our world works the way it does. Science breaks things down into their component parts, studies the parts, looks for causal relationships between them, and declares scientific findings to be facts. There are basic assumptions the scientist makes as he or she practices this system. For example, *reductionism* is the belief that things can be better understood if they are broken down and studied in parts. *Determinism* is the belief that everything that happens has been caused by something else. And the grandest assumption of all is that everything that happens can be perceived by the human mind. The scientist cannot prove that any of these assumptions are true. How can we prove that everything about our complex world is humanly comprehensible? To disprove the opposite, we would need to have someone with a nonhuman brain explain to us what exists outside our human realm of comprehension; so far, we haven't had contact with such a form of intelligent life.

Nevertheless, scientists simply accept these assumptions on faith, the same way that a fundamentalist Christian accepts the Bible as the literal word of God. Scientists need such assumptions in order to be able to interpret the findings of their systems as being valid. Considering how much stock type A individuals put into figuring out and controlling the external world, it appears that they are actually people of tremendous faith!

Type A individuals may also get hung up concerning science and religion because of worries about being "right" or "best"—they must come out on top or else they will perceive of themselves as being "losers," "wrong," or substandard in some other way. But there is no "best" or "right" when it comes to these systems. They both have their usefulness, in different ways. I would rather trust the system of science when I'm trying to figure out how to get my roses to bloom more proficiently, as well as which psychotherapeutic intervention will most likely help a suicidal patient. But in the arena of feeling at peace with myself and experiencing oneness with my world, I would much rather take into account the more ambiguously defined leanings and feelings of my inner spirit.

Discovering the Spirit

Relating to our spiritual selves happens in the present. Type A individuals, in their pursuit of the never-ending list of future goals and preoccupation with injuries of the past, may not be aware of their spiritual selves. The first task of healing the spirit is, therefore, to find it.

There are many different techniques for seeking our inner selves, but the end results do not differ very significantly, at least in terms of spiritual connectedness. The process has many different labels, depending on the philosophy upon which the technique is based. It is beyond the scope of this section to give detailed explanations of all of the various ways to pursue introspection. Instead, I am presenting a review of some of the more salient techniques and providing references for those who wish to pursue a technique further.

One of the most pervasive and longstanding forms of self-introspection is prayer or meditation, as taught by

Judeo-Christian faiths. The goal of such prayer is to know oneself better by knowing God better. Some people will meditate on a piece of scripture until they find congruence between its teachings and their own inner spirit. Others will try to empty their minds as much as possible so that God's will or personalized teachings can enter. Others seek out what they know they specifically need, such as meditating on the concept of God's love until they feel joined with God's love and at peace with themselves.

The best resource for learning about prayer or meditation is your pastor, priest, or rabbi. Most likely he or she will have favorite books on prayer that are consistent with the faith you have chosen to practice. If you do not have a church affiliation, your local Christian bookstore will most likely have an entire rack devoted to books on prayer. Remember that you are looking for a book on *how* to pray, rather than on *what* to pray about. Or perhaps you may decide that now is the time to find your own church or synagogue and learn more about faith in general.

Another form of introspection is called the "relaxation response."[9] This system, taught by Herbert Benson, borrows meditation techniques from Eastern religions. The meditator sits quietly in a comfortable position, closes his or her eyes, and progressively relaxes the various parts of the body. The meditator focuses on the feeling of breathing and concentrates on a word or phrase. The specific word or phrase is not important; it simply provides a reference point to which the meditator can return when distracting thoughts begin to interfere. The process continues for about fifteen or twenty minutes. Afterwards, the meditator feels refreshed and renewed. With repeated practice, it is possible to access this feeling of being at peace just by thinking about it.

Joan Borysenko calls this feeling "mindfulness."[10] She describes it as being "mindful" of the present, without letting concerns from the past and worries about the future intrude into one's sense of peace and joy. Her book describes how to meditate and provides exercises for encouraging relaxation as well as a system for emotional healing.

Eugene Gendlin describes a style of introspection that he calls "focusing."[11] Instead of emptying everything from the present, focusing is a process of zeroing in on a specific problem and working it through on an emotional level. The person "clears a space" internally, acknowledging and setting aside all ongoing concerns, and picks one particular difficulty upon which to focus. The "felt sense" about the problem is the object of the focusing, rather than stewing over the various possible solutions and ramifications of the problem. The concentration continues as the person finds a label for what he or she senses and meditates on what might be causing the felt sense, which eventually produces a feeling of an "emotional shift," resulting in a sense of healing.

As I said earlier, there is no one best way of finding your spirit; the best system is the one that works best for you. Pick the one that fits in with your own beliefs. If you can't decide, figure out which one *feels* the most comfortable. By all means, do not be afraid to seek out help from others while learning the process.

Knowing the Spirit

Once we come into contact with our spiritual selves, what might we find there? It is probably safe to assume that everyone will find something different. However, there seems to be a commonality among these differences that everyone finds. Its theme is a vital connectedness to others.

One major philosophy of psychology calls this feeling of connection "social interest." The meaning of social interest is perhaps better explained by looking at all the alternative ways the original German word *Gemeinschaftgefuhl* can be translated: "social feeling, community feeling, fellow feeling, sense of solidarity, communal intuition, community interest, social sense, and social interest."[12] In a nutshell, social interest is the feeling of connectedness with and empathy and concern we have for our fellow human beings. It is also described as being a tool that we use as a mechanism for our own personal striving toward growth.

Perhaps it is the discovery of this internal tool that resulted in Friedman's type A patients' becoming more productive after treatment. As they became more internally aware, they became more sensitive to the needs and desires of others around them. By tailoring their own efforts to mesh with the interests of others, they were more able to see their efforts succeed. Working with others does not entail simply diagnosing for yourself what you think the world needs and then foisting your efforts upon it. It means using intuition and sensitivity, as well as having a genuine interest in the well-being of those around you, blended in such a way that efforts on both sides reach a congruency of striving even in the midst of disagreement and apparent failure to find solutions to difficulties. Eventual courses of action are more likely to leave all feeling satisfied, since such action was born of a oneness of striving among many, rather than one type A running roughshod over everyone else. Such continuing successes strengthen us, as following through on our internal sense is reinforced by the results of its worldly striving.

The major religions also see connectedness to others through concern and interest as being vital. When Jesus was asked which commandment was most important, he said that one should love God. He quickly added that one should love others and oneself as well. Confucius made a related statement, stating that the one saying that can continuously pervade our daily living was to avoid doing to others what you would not want done to yourself. The teachings of Buddha instruct that love is the keystone to the three other "Sublime Abodes" of compassion, sympathetic joy, and equanimity. The necessity of a positive unity with others is so pervasive that it apparently influenced all of these important religious leaders, in spite of their living in different parts of the world during different eras.

While finding our spiritual connectedness is one benefit of knowing our spirits, the greatest joy to be found is the sense of peace and appreciation for living that can be found only within the spirit. Rabbi Harold Kushner describes this state of being in *When All You've Ever Wanted Isn't Enough.* The book is a study of Ecclesiastes, a story about a hapless Old Testament character who kept on striving but just couldn't seem to get it right. He sought after such entities as power, wealth, and wisdom, and succeeded in fighting his way to the top of all of them. Yet, he was still not satisfied. His victories were hollow, and his attainments provided only fleeting joy. Once his goals were met, they ceased to have value.

Until he finally realized that life is living, not attaining, his life was meaningless. Kushner encourages us to fill our days with moments that gratify us—not in a selfish or disorganized way, but in a manner that allows us to do what we must, yet appreciate and enjoy the doing of it. He shares his observations of the wisdom found by Ecclesiastes in the following passage:

> When we stop searching for the Great Answer, the Immortal Deed which will give our lives ongoing meaning, and instead concentrate on filling our individual days with moments that gratify us, then we will find the only possible answer to the question, "What is life about?" It is not about writing great books, amassing great wealth, achieving great power. It is about loving and being loved. It is about enjoying your food and sitting in the sun rather than rushing through lunch and hurrying back to the office. It is about savoring the beauty of moments that don't last, the sunsets, the leaves turning color, the rare moments of true human communication. It is about savoring them rather than missing out on them because we are so busy and they will not hold still until we get around to them. The author of Ecclesiastes spent most of his life

looking for the Grand Solution, the Big Answer to the Big Question, only to learn after wasting many years that trying to find one Big Answer to the problem of living is like trying to eat one Big Meal so that you will never have to worry about being hungry again. There is no Answer, but there are answers: love and the joy of working, and the simple pleasures of food and fresh clothes, the little things that get lost and trampled in the search for the Grand Solution to the Problem of Life and emerge, like the proverbial bluebird of happiness, only when we have stopped searching. When we come to that stage in our lives when we are less able to accomplish but more able to enjoy, we will have attained the wisdom that Ecclesiastes finally found after so many false starts and disappointments.[13]

Living this philosophy can embellish every facet of healing a type A life-style. Emotionally, it removes the torment of "Am I good enough yet?" and replaces it with the self-acceptance of "I simply am, and this is good." Interpersonally, it dismantles the casting of others as entities who either fulfill or impede our desires, and transforms them into beloved fellow sojourners. Physically, such a philosophy reduces the chances of stress-produced ailments and values life so dearly that we could not consider letting our bodies go to waste due to neglect. And spiritually, it provides a sense of peace and contentment that not even the highest mound of accomplishments could ever replace.

This is the philosophy of a healthy achiever. It is the philosophy I would like to see this book encourage in every parent, child, teacher, counselor, social worker, therapist, or anyone else who plays a part in the arena of molding children's achievement styles. Young children do have difficulty grasping philosophies like this one, since their thought lives still deal in the concrete, rather than the abstract. However, we can begin to lay the foundation for a healthy life philosophy as we parent them as well as weed out some of the less productive interactions our own type A styles might encourage.

Chapter Six

Helping the Child

There is a limit to how much we can count on influencing our children's eventual achieving style. Parenting comprises a significant, but small, portion of those influences that will form a child's character. One of the more basic factors determining a child's personality is his or her biological temperament. Children appear to be biologically programmed toward certain tendencies, such as being shy and timid, or sociable and outgoing; there are other factors as well.[1] The culture in which the child is immersed will play a significant role; birth order, the world condition during the child's development, role models, and even chance itself all affect a child's eventual philosophy, thoughts, feelings, and subsequent behaviors.

We cannot change our child's basic neurochemistry, at least not at this juncture. Nor can we change a child's birth order, peer history, culture, or the chance situations and role models a child might stumble across. But we can change the way we parent. Research has shown that even children born excessively inhibited can learn to rise above their temperament as they go through the socialization process, adapting to their surroundings and inner tendencies.[2] This suggests that, as parents, we can provide a tremendous service for our children by encouraging them toward healthy achieving, even when they appear to have the type A temperament from day one. It also suggests that we can unwittingly put our children at risk by creating an environment that promotes dysfunctional adaptation by otherwise even-tempered children. This chapter looks at ways we can assist our children in becoming healthy achievers and avoid directing them toward a type A life-style.

If you recall, type A behavior begins with low self-esteem, after which the unbalanced type A life-style is learned through modeling, reward systems, and active training by parents and others. The remainder of this chapter is divided into three sections: promoting self-worth, promoting a balanced life-style (as opposed to a type A life-style), and additional helpful hints.

If you are a rip-roaring type A, some of these interventions may be extremely difficult for you to reconcile with your own type A reacting. Make use of the techniques described in the last chapter while interacting with your child. Mediate your impatience, angry responding, and domineering tendencies with tactics such as leaving the room, counting to ten, diaphragmatic breathing, the rubber-band technique and other forms of thought stopping, restructuring your thinking patterns, and using assertive behavior. What better place to practice these techniques than at home, while you are with the people who care about you most?

PROMOTING SELF-WORTH

Foster your child's sense of self-acceptance. Endeavor to help your child feel accepted just for the person he or she is. Children can attain a firm sense of identity through feeling accepted. We can show that we are accepting of them by demonstrating "unconditional positive regard." In other words, show positive feelings toward your child at every opportunity. A spontaneous loving smile, an unexpected hug, saying "I love you" for no special reason, and telling your child that you noticed something nice about him or her all send the message that your child is acceptable.

Limit or avoid: Try not to attach acceptance to achievement. It's okay to show affection or approval of your child when he or she does something well; just don't make this the only time you show positive regard. Otherwise the child learns that acceptance of oneself is something one must earn. Likewise, during discipline do not become rejecting of the child. Make it clear that you reject inappropriate behavior, but that you still love the child.

Praise your child's efforts. Praise all efforts, even the ones that are not successful. We do not have complete control over the outcome of our efforts, but we are in control of how hard we try. The fact that we make an effort, in the face of not knowing whether or not we will succeed, is a demonstration of our courage and strength of character. Reinforce this in your child by letting him or her know that you took note of the part of the outcome that represents who the child is: "Good effort!" "Nice try!" "You sure worked hard on that one." "You were looking great out there today" (when the child's efforts have actually failed).

Limit or avoid: Do not attach praise solely to achievement. Likewise, limit your criticisms of your children's efforts. If they are not trying, they already know it, and your reminding them of it only implies that they are not okay unless they make their best effort on absolutely everything. Children make choices concerning how they will expend their energy the same as anyone else does; these personal choices need to be validated, not criticized. Putting full effort into absolutely everything would guarantee development of the fast burn-out track of the type A achiever. Support and guide them through this priority-setting process. And focusing solely on how a child could have done better—even when the child came out on top—should be outlawed, unless the child has specifically requested such input. Otherwise, limit such comments to times specified for learning or training, not during times the child is trying to demonstrate his or her skill for you.

Encourage self-confidence. Demonstrate confidence in your children's ability to handle situations. Showing confidence in them encourages their ability to have confidence in themselves: "I'm sure you'll find a solution." "I knew you could do it." "This looks like something you might be able to help us with."

Limit or avoid: Avoid undermining children's confidence in themselves. Doing things for children that they can do for themselves, excessive criticism, trying to win every disagreement, insisting on winning every game played with them, constantly telling them what to do and how and when to do it, making their choices for them, and blowing up at children when they fail to perform all undermine children's self-confidence.

Validate your child's ideas and feelings. Children need to recognize that their ideas are important and worthwhile, as part of valuing themselves as persons. Take the time to listen when they want to share a new idea or express an exciting or distressing feeling. Help them learn to express anger assertively, rather than aggressively, by both modeling it for them and using direct instruction.

Limit or avoid: Do not put down childish ideas just because they are immature. Of course, children's ideas are immature; they come from children! Likewise, do not try to put a lid over your child's feelings just because they are unpleasant for you to experience. Feelings are natural and normal, and if you react unacceptingly when your child expresses them, he or she will figure there is something wrong with him or her. There is never a good reason for ridiculing a child's feelings.

Allow children to choose the activities they wish to pursue. Children need to be the ones who choose their extracurricular activities, so they will feel free and competent enough to be able to pursue their interests. Establish a realistic, specific time span during which the child must stick to the chosen activity, and afterwards let the child decide whether or not the activity is worth continuing.

Limit or avoid: Avoid picking your children's activities for them, since this undermines their confidence in their ability to pick out and pursue what really interests them. As type A parents, we might choose to put children into activities that we ourselves wish we had mastered, or that we perceive as having status value, rather than something our children would truly enjoy. And, remember, just because a child turns out to be good at something does not mean that activity must be pursued. This would be true only if our worth depended on the roles we play, since we would then want to pursue roles that made us look superior. Just because a child is good at something does not mean that the activity is something he or she enjoys. Usually only an overly coerced child is likely to have trouble making himself or herself find something to do, and if overcoercion is the problem, we should be addressing our parenting style, rather than using our child's symptoms as an excuse to take over his or her choices.

Provide consistent and fair discipline. Be very clear about what you expect from each child and enforce your expectations. Be fair about how you deliver discipline—let your children know where the boundaries are ahead of time, before you go about trying to enforce them. In this way, children can succeed in meeting your expectations and feel good about their ability to do so.

Limit or avoid: Do not let things go because you do not wish to interrupt your own activity, waiting until things get completely out of hand, and then blow up. When you enforce boundaries intermittently, your children become confused about where they really are, which undermines their ability to succeed. The child sees such "failures" as evidence of his or her own inadequacy, rather than as the expected result of disciplinary inconsistency.

PROMOTING A BALANCED LIFE-STYLE

Help children learn to appreciate the present. Talk to your children in terms of the present. Ask them to describe what they are doing as they play, if you can do so without being too intrusive: "What are you playing now? How fun!" Comment on your own feelings at a given moment: "Isn't this fun?" "That sun feels warm." "I feel sad about the character in this story." "I feel good while I'm doing my best." "I like just sitting with you right now."

Limit or avoid: Limit the amount of time you spend emphasizing past errors or discussing future goals. They are important topics for discussion, but continual harping on them draws unnecessarily from the amount of time the child can get to know how he or she feels in the present. Since life occurs only in the present, overemphasis on the past and future can stifle the child's ability to experience life.

Foster your children's natural sense of empathy. Label your children's feelings concerning others as you see them emerge: "So you feel bad about Jennifer's being sick." "I see you feel good about sharing your toys with Jason." You can serve the same purpose by verbalizing your own feelings concerning others: "I'm glad Nathan got a new bike; he has wanted one for a long time." "I feel bad for that lady trying to hang on to all of those items. I think I'll let her get in line ahead of me." Emphasizing feelings and concerns about others provides a model of valuing others, which will aid your children as they develop attitudes concerning their own relationships with others. When children misbehave, point out how their actions affect others, especially concerning how victims of their misbehavior must feel.

Limit or Avoid: Steer away from power-oriented discipline, like reward and punishment, whenever possible. These forms of discipline teach children to look outside of themselves for direction, rather than inside for personal, empathy-based direction.[3] Do not encourage the idea that winning, achieving, and dominating are more important than another person's feelings, either through modeling or direct instruction. Winning is nice, but not if you are brutal toward others in how you go about doing it. Achieving is great, but not if you squash people in your path and ignore your significant others in the process. Dominating is unnecessary and reflects our insecurities more than it reflects strengths. Being directive during a task while in a position of authority is one thing; always insisting that things be done your way in all settings and under all circumstances is not adaptive, and it wreaks havoc on your personal life and cardiovascular system.

Help children learn how to express caring and affection. Most children are spontaneously affectionate. They run up and want to be hugged; they come and sit in your lap; and they even verbally express feelings of affection toward parents without any special encouragement. Be accepting of these emotional overtures, as well as take the time to receive them, so that your child will know that his or her spontaneous affection is appropriate and desirable. Model your own affection toward others—let your children see Daddy hug Mommy; say "I love you" to other family members—illustrate for your children that you see them and others as being worthy of affection and that it is desirable to both feel it and express it.

Limit or avoid: Avoid criticizing, dominating, and blowing up at people. This is the antithesis of showing affection toward others and will lead to your child's not trusting your attempts at being affectionate. Avoid domination-related "affection," such as tickling or wrestling a child to the ground. Try two-way cooperative affection, like hugging, sitting together, a pat on the back, or holding hands, instead.

Support children in their ability to choose friends. Strengthen your child's confidence in his or her ability to form friendships and maintain them. Comment on the positive attributes of your child's friends, or what you see your child liking about his or her friends. Empathize with your child as he or she struggles with frustrations concerning friendships, and express confidence that your child will be able to work things out one way or another.

Limit or avoid: Do not choose your children's friends for them, no matter how much utilitarian value you see in a prospective friend. That is not what friendships are for; they are for fulfilling our need for interpersonal closeness, not for use during our various corporate climbs. Children need friends who are companions, with whom they can share the frustrations and delights of growing and learning. Their own inner spirits will guide them toward finding their "kindred spirits." When children make friends who are significantly bad influences, they will usually terminate the relationships themselves unless the parent has turned the issue into a power struggle, in which case children may maintain ill-advised friendships forever just to protect the autonomy of their friend making. If the situation becomes a matter of life and death, such as drug involvement, crime rings, or prostitution, by all means step in. Otherwise, let children find the peer group with whom they can feel spiritually joined.

Help children learn to focus on the enjoyment of an activity, rather than on winning or losing. When you talk with your children about their activities, ask *qualitative* questions about them: "How did you like it?" "What was the best part?" "Who else got to play with you?" "Tell me about how this game is played." "How did you make this?"

Limit or avoid: Avoid emphasizing the typical *quantitative* questions of the type A achiever: "Did you win?" "How good a grade did you get?" "Where did you place in the group?" Children will share these sorts of things spontaneously if they are important to them.

Emphasize a child's personal achievements, as opposed to material achievements. Place the lion's share of your praise within the realm of the child's personal victories, raising his or her skill level—as in learning to ride a bike or overcoming a personal limitation—like getting up the nerve to give a report in front of the class. These accomplishments represent true personal growth and achievement and do not get in the way of or depend on anyone else's growth and achievement.

Limit or avoid: Do not compare your child's achievements to any other child's. This teaches the child that his or her accomplishments matter only in terms of how they measure up to others' accomplishments. Nobody will ever exceed everybody else, and comparisons direct the child toward an achievement life-style of always looking at people who have accomplished more. This leads to the child's feeling that his or her efforts and achievements are inadequate as well as an inability to enjoy the process of personal achievement.

Teach power-sharing, rather than domination. Teaching children to power-share, rather than dominate, helps them learn to value the needs and rights of others. Allow children to see you and your spouse go about making decisions in an even-sided manner. If this concept is foreign to you, the general rule of thumb is that when you can't come to an agreement on important decisions, you take turns getting the final say on decisions of that magnitude. Share the power of decision making with your children when possible; get their input before you make executive decisions, or let them have turns making simple family decisions (what to have for dinner, which TV program to watch, the evening leisure activity, and the like).

Limit or avoid: Avoid trying to run the whole show. Remember that making their choices for them models just the sort of domineering tactics you would like them to avoid, since these tactics undermine interpersonal relationships and tend to raise one's blood pressure as well.

Monitor the amount of time your child spends on academic-achievement activities. Children should not spend more than a couple of hours a day on homework; grade-school children should spend no more than an hour. Otherwise, they do not have time for play, developing social relationships, and finding ways to relax. Play is part of the "work" of childhood, and if children are spending an excessive amount of time on academics, they can become developmentally stunted in other important areas. If your child seems preoccupied with academic success, emphasize along the way that you love him or her no matter what his or her grades are and that there are other things to enjoy in life besides school activities. Introduce play yourself when children seem hesitant—offer to go on a bike ride with them, play a board game, watch a TV program together, or engage in any of the noncompetitive pastimes listed later in this chapter.

Limit or avoid: Do not set up academic achievement and winning competitions as the do-all and be-all of life. Getting good or average grades rather than the best grades might limit some options down the line, but being the best academically or in some other competitive field is not worth it if your child has to sacrifice other areas of development in order to attain that status.

ADDITIONAL HELPFUL HINTS

Don't let your expectations of your children allow you to fault them when they do not do as well as you think they should. We do not even know what our own potentials are, let alone what our children's potentials might be. Would we fault a child because his or her eyes aren't as blue as we would have expected? Just as children can't control their eye color, they cannot control their innate potential. Telling them that you expect them to achieve more than they may actually be able to deliver crumbles their self-esteem. If they really do seem to be achieving at a level far below what you have seen them accomplish, search for reasons why: a problem at school, feeling pressured, a recent emotional upset, a previously undetected learning disability, a sight or hearing problem, or perhaps even feeling unchallenged in their current learning environment. Find the problem and resolve it, rather than telling your children that they aren't trying hard enough when it's impossible to know for sure that they really are not meeting their potential.

Lavishing praise over everything your children do puts too much emphasis on their accomplishments. Give lavish praise only when you see a behavior or accomplishment that is exceptional, or that you really like yourself. Excessive praise over every little thing makes children feel as though they must always come up with something exceptional to be worthy of your attention.

Divide up household chores with the stance that they are a collection of things that the whole family needs to do. Thus every family member will take part in doing them. This helps children to feel useful, competent, and able to contribute toward the care of themselves and others. Taking a stance that says, "I am in charge, and you are going to do this" minimizes such a team effort.

Avoid doing things over for your children. This teaches them that their efforts are substandard or not worthwhile.

Remember that it is all right to seek perfection; just don't set it up as a standard that you expect your children to meet. Only God can create perfection; human beings cannot.

Set realistic goals for your children. You cannot create a "superior" child, no matter how hard you try. Children simply turn out to be whoever they are, in spite of our efforts. Stand back and give them room; foster their own attempts at goal setting, and they will learn to meet their potentials.

Don't ask your children to "perform" their gifts and talents for company. Such an emphasis teaches them that their significance in the world depends on showing how smart or talented they are, rather than their having value just for being human beings. If children want to perform, they will be sure to let you know of such a desire, one way or the other. Furthermore, children will have difficulty getting along with others if they have been trained to hold center stage in the world. How much time do you like to spend around people who always insist on being the center of attention?

Provide opportunities for your children to learn. This differs from choosing their activities for them. Take them to the library, but let them decide what sorts of books or other materials they would like to pursue. Take them to the zoo or museum, but let them direct themselves toward what interests them—rather than rushing from display to display so that you can be sure to see everything, and in the least possible time! Purchase children's encyclopedias and other series of books that provide exposure to broad areas of learning, so your children can browse through them at their leisure and zero in on whatever catches their interest. In this way you help your children learn to take advantage of their opportunities. Bob Keeshan, better known as "Captain Kangaroo," traces the origins of his beliefs about childrearing in his autobiography *Growing Up Happy.*[4] He points out that his successes in life were not due to being "lucky"—there is no such thing as luck. However, we do get many opportunities in our lives, which we can either act upon or ignore. Happiness and good fortune occur when we bring our own abilities to bear on those opportunities that chance provides, and make wise choices concerning which opportunities we will pursue. Our children need practice in choosing and taking advantage of their opportunities.

When your children seem discouraged, verbalize the philosophy of the healthy achiever, as it pertains to the situation. A frustration is actually a new adventure and a potential learning experience; a person who disappoints us in some way is also a human being, reacting as human beings do; the world does have its drawbacks, but we can handle ourselves in the world anyway; and we are all special and valuable, even when our efforts do not succeed.

Children need the courage to try new things without the fear of failure. Don't let your own type A need to criticize or other domineering behaviors oversensitize your children to failure. Otherwise, you paralyze their willingness to try something new, no matter how fun or interesting it might look.

Children need to spend time in activities that are noncompetitive, cooperative in nature, and/or creative and skill-oriented, so that recreational and interpersonal activities do not end up sucked into the achievement vacuum. Below is a list of activities you can do with your child that need not be competitive. But remember, just about anything can be turned into a competition—even something as innocent as learning Bible verses can be turned into competing Bible quiz teams. Guard against this; there are already enough competitive activities in our culture to teach our children how to compete.

"Just for the Fun of It" Activities

Have a sing-a-long
Read aloud
Make up stories
Paint, create from clay or other artistic mediums
Take dance lessons—ballroom, folk, square, modern, ballet, etc.
Go on a hike
Go swimming
Go camping
Bake cookies
Go on a bike ride
Go for a walk in the park or along the beach
Have a picnic in the mountains
Take a bus ride downtown
Give a puppet show
Construct and fly a kite
Set up a lemonade stand
Go to the playground
Write letters of concern to your representative in Congress
Rent a videotape
Plant a garden
Do needlecraft, such as knitting, needlepoint, etc.
Do photography
Try tie-dying and puff-painting
Collect and learn about stamps, coins, shells, rocks, baseball cards, etc.
Color in coloring books
Listen to classical music
Go on a trail ride
Visit libraries, museums, and zoos
Do woodworking
Do something together for charity
Go fishing
Learn basket weaving
Study a foreign language
Start a scrapbook
Go window shopping

Put on a play
Learn calligraphy
Go sledding
Cut out paper dolls
Make a videotape
Practice Tai Chi
Go whale watching or on some other such tour
Climb a tree
Take a yoga class together
Hide some buried treasure and make a map for it
See a play or concert
Go sailing
Lie in the grass and watch the clouds—what do they look like?
Build and maintain a birdhouse or bird feeder
Work on your family's genealogy
Jump in mud puddles
Make candles
Make funny faces
Learn to do magic tricks
Go for a train ride
Do chemistry experiments
Raise gerbils
Learn to use a boomerang
Fold paper airplanes
Put puzzles together
Roll down the hill
Go roller skating
Walk the dog
Learn yo-yo tricks
Build houses out of cards, popsicle sticks, or toothpicks
Carve soap
Release helium-filled balloons with secret messages
Get an ant farm
Build a fort
Make doll clothes
Learn the Morse code

The following charts summarize the "do's and don'ts" for parenting a healthy achiever.

To Encourage Healthy Achieving:	Limit or Avoid:
Self-esteem Variables	
Show unconditional acceptance of your child	Do not attach acceptance to achievement or good behavior
Praise all efforts, even unsuccessful ones	Do not attach praise only to achievement; limit criticism of efforts
Show confidence in your child's abilities	Avoid undermining self-confidence by taking over
Validate your child's ideas and feelings	Do not put down immature thoughts and feelings
Let your child choose his or her extracurricular activities	Avoid picking your child's activities
Provide fair and consistent discipline	Avoid whimsical or sporadic discipline
Balanced Life-style Variables	
Help your child learn to appreciate the present	Limit emphasis on past errors and future goals
Foster your child's natural sense of empathy	Steer away from power-oriented discipline
Help your child learn to express caring and affection	Manage your anger and domineering tendencies
Support your child in his or her ability to choose friends	Do not choose your child's friends for him or her
Ask qualitative questions about your child's activities	Avoid quantitative questions about your child's activities
Emphasize your child's personal, rather than material, achievements	Do not compare your child's achievements to those of other children
Teach your child power-sharing	Avoid keeping all the power for yourself
Monitor the amount of time your child spends in academics	Do not push academics as the be-all of living

To Encourage Healthy Achieving:
(continued)

Other Hints

When your child has difficulties, help find and overcome obstacles

Save lavish praise for that which is truly exceptional

Use a team responsibility model for handling household chores

Be respectful of the results of immature efforts

Treat perfection as a standard toward which to aim

Set realistic goals for your child

Let your child decide when to share gifts and talents with others

Expand opportunities for learning

Verbalize the philosophy of the healthy achiever

Encourage your child to try new things

Help your child find activities that are noncompetitive, cooperative, and/or creative or skill-oriented

Limit or Avoid:
(continued)

Do not fault your child if he or she isn't meeting your perception of his or her "potential"

Do not pour excessive praise over everything

Avoid a domineering stance toward assignment of chores

Do not do things over for your child

Do not treat perfection as a standard expected to be met

Avoid unrealistic expectations

Do not ask your child to "perform" for company

Avoid narrowing opportunities by pushing your own preferences

Play down the philosophy of the type A achiever

Do not create a fear of failure by criticizing and ridiculing new efforts

Discourage the type A stance during competitive and achievement-oriented activity

Chapter Seven

Western Culture and Childrearing

We live in a fast-paced, hard-driving, success-oriented culture. There is nothing wrong with success. Likewise, there is nothing wrong with doing something quickly or with intensity, at least in reasonable doses. But our culture seems to have set this up as the daily norm. Unless we are constantly pushing toward our full potential, striving toward the highest peaks, and crossing the widest rivers, our culture often gives us the message that something is wrong with us. In other words, our culture can play the roles of encouraging low self-esteem in our children—the cornerstone of type A behavior—and underemphasizing the joy of just "being," to overemphasize plummeting oneself toward success—the model of type A striving.

INDUSTRY AND THE FAMILY

The introduction of industry played a significant role in our childrearing practices. Before the Industrial Revolution, the family was less divided in its role functions. Women and children were more likely to be involved in the family's source of income, such as farming, various forms of craft work, and running small businesses. Men played a greater role in the rearing of children, since children often grew up as apprentices in their fathers' livelihoods.

As our culture became more industrially oriented, family roles became more sharply defined. Someone had to bring in an income, and someone had to take care of the children. Since the workplace moved from the home to the factory, the breadwinner could not simultaneously provide child care. Thus a sharp division occurred. Men, who on the basis of brute strength were able to outperform women in the predominantly manual labor of the day, were generally elected as the persons who would go out and earn a living. Women, who were already tied to children because of pregnancy and nursing, were assigned the role of raising the children. Other cultural biases and influences played a role in this division as well, but the end result was still the extreme role definitions we have seen in recent times.[1]

Being assigned to taking care of children was actually a boon to the status of women. Everyone agreed that the rearing of children was important, and entrusting something so important to women has raised the dignity of women to greater heights in our culture than anywhere else in the world.[2] Women were able to feel better about themselves because they could play such an important role.

Likewise, there were benefits for men in this system. They no longer had to deal with the responsibility for and pressure involved in trying to get by on their own; their hours were finite, giving them free time to pursue other interests; and they received the dependable reward of a steady paycheck. They learned to feel good because of the success they had in the role of provider.

Unfortunately, somewhere along the line roles ceased to be what we do and became who we are. "This *feels* good" has slowly become replaced by "I *am* good because I succeed at this." Our culture has been persistently introducing new facets to our society that play on the concept of working hard in our roles in order to be able to feel good about ourselves. Even advertising jingles have capitalized on this notion: "You deserve a break today" implies that you are constantly working hard at something (or at least you should be) and that feeling good should come after you have earned it.

PARENTING, WESTERN STYLE

The end result of this cultural formulation is that women have been assigned the role of mothering and have been encouraged to believe that they are okay as persons if they have succeeded in raising good children. In recent years, as men have been reinvolving themselves in basic parenting, they too are experiencing an increasing tie between their self-esteem and their children's ability to perform. The fact that parents are only one major influence among many in a child's development seems to have gotten lost and trampled in the stampede toward proving parental worthiness. We all take pride in our children's achievements, but neither our children nor their achievements have anything to do with our worth as human beings.

Our culture has responded in many ways to this unreasonable fear. Look at how childrearing manuals have proliferated in the last few decades. They used to be rare! Their appearance is caused in part by our information explosion and the struggle to get new information out to where it can be used. But an additional reason they have become so successful is fear: "If I don't raise perfect kids, it means I'm a crummy parent, and that means I have no value." Thus our book purchases abound, which may be good, if we come across material that eases our fears and helps us with our parenting. But it can also be damaging, in that we might also get hold of material that is "fringy," extremist, or outside of the bounds of what science is actually telling us, as well as further encouraging us to believe that our worth is wrapped up in how well we parent.

Parents also seem to be having more difficulty waiting for children to arrive at the age at which they can be expected to achieve various milestones. The "superbaby" philosophy is still in full swing. Parents seek training and information on how to get their baby to read, perform mathematical calculations, and obtain "encyclopedic knowledge." Whole lines of toys have been developed that are supposed to help babies develop basic skills more quickly, in spite of the fact that such skills will emerge on their own just by the process of a baby's natural exploration, special toys or no special toys. Preschools are putting a greater and greater emphasis on teaching the ABC's and 123's, which used to be a part of grade-school curriculum, and some of these more "progressive" schools have entrance competition rivaling that of elite universities. Parents try to get their children into grade school early, in the hope of hurrying along the process of creating a "superior" child.

In spite of the fact that these parents are ostensibly trying to create an advanced child, they may in fact be doing just the opposite. Children have only so many days, so much energy, and so much attention available for funneling into basic development. If there is an overemphasis on development of academic and other selected skills, other aspects of development—such as emotional, interpersonal, and physical development—will be left deficient. These other aspects are every bit as crucial to a child's ability to succeed as academics are; yet, they can easily end up underdeveloped because of parents' misplaced emphases.

There is no harm in giving your baby educational toys. But if you place one baby in a playpen full of educational toys and turn another baby loose in a baby-proofed home, guess which one is likely to develop more skills? It will be the one turned loose in the "average expectable environment," not the one who has been restricted and directed toward a limited realm of play.

Prematurely pushing a child into the world of academia can also be damaging. James Uphoff is critical of such maneuvers: "Memorization looks good, sounds good, allows parents to brag their heads off, but if we're talking about rote behavior, there are a number of animal species that can be taught rote behavior."[3] He goes on to point out what happens to children whose average expectable environment has been sacrificed to the god of achievement:

> The kids who have lacked quantity-quality play later have been found to be lacking in creative-thought ability, the ability to make decisions and the ability to cope with emotional stress. . . . Another study found these children having far more anti-social behavior incidences at ages 15, 16. We're talking about vandalism, fighting, truancy, disrespect.[4]

And according to the American Academy of Pediatrics, more and more stress-related symptoms have been turning up in small children.[5] Could this also be due to the fast track upon which they are being thrust?

Starting children in school too early can have detrimental effects that follow children around for the rest of their lives. James Uphoff, June Gilmore, and Rosemarie Huber describe the potential ill effects of starting children early in their book, *Summer Children*.[6] The fact that a child may be bright does not mean that he or she is physically, socially, or emotionally ready for the rigors of academic learning. As Uphoff and his colleagues reviewed the research on such children, they found a number of difficulties experienced by children who began kindergarten before the age of five and a half. Younger children are not as advanced in their motor skills, vision development, and attention span as older children. Thus problems develop as they are less able to stay in their seats and listen, have difficulty managing a pencil, and reverse symbols. Emotionally, they may not be ready for the types of cooperative interactions involved with the school setting. The result is children who have difficulty getting along with their classmates as well as being more likely to be described by teachers as having emotional problems. Further along in their educational experience, early starters are more likely to be classified as learning disabled, to repeat a grade, to experience low scholastic achievement, and to lack leadership ability.

Difficulties can even follow children into high school. One study looked at the performance of advanced-placement high school students in a research task. The task involved the ability to plan, organize, provide self-discipline, and meet deadlines. In spite of the fact that all of the students were exceptionally bright, the students earning the lowest grades were the early starters.

One of the most devastating results of enrolling children before they are ready concerns their own developing beliefs about how successful they can expect to be in the world. Early starters tend to end up with lower self-images, and why shouldn't they? They recognize that they are smaller than their peers, less coordinated, less able to handle a classroom situation, and have to work twice as hard to get the same grades. Under those circumstances, who wouldn't suffer a blow to self-esteem? In one instance, a higher incidence of suicide attempts was found among early starters. Is this really so surprising?

In view of this body of research, it appears that pushing children into school early encourages type A behavior in two ways. First, it puts children into a setting where they really do not measure up in terms of their ability to succeed, thus helping to set up the cornerstone of low self-esteem. Second, as they try to compensate for their disadvantage, they learn to work twice as hard as others to get the same results, thus learning to busy themselves with overkill in their achievement efforts.

The bottom line is that we as parents need to ask

ourselves about our priorities. On one hand, we will create a higher level of status for ourselves and our children if we rush them along into trendy preschools and push for early placement in grade school. But at what cost to our children's overall development? Is that tiny bit of status worth sacrificing our children's future attitudes toward their sense of worth, toward achievement, and toward life in general? And at what cost will it be to ourselves, if we are simply using our children to create one more external measure of our worth, and thereby undermining our ability to see that we have inner worth no matter how our children might perform? We are all losers when we try to push our children toward overachievement.

We can, however, enhance our children's learning through alternative methods. In *The Hurried Child*, David Elkind points out that even those who made tremendous contributions to our society did not necessarily have special extracurricular training. He illustrates his point with the biographies of Eleanor Roosevelt, Albert Einstein, and Thomas Edison—all of whom missed a lot of formal education as children, and in fact were viewed by others as having deficiencies. He also discusses a study in which, out of a group of four hundred eminent people, three-fifths showed a strong dislike for formal education, even though four-fifths of them showed exceptional talent. Elkind questions why we would expect such children to want even more formal education at home. However, he cites another study that found that the home was indeed an important element in the development of gifted children, insofar as the parents of such children appeared to have a love of learning themselves. He goes on to make the following suggestion:

> Parents who love learning will create a stimulating environment for children, which is far more beneficial to them than specific instruction. Parents who fill the house with books, paintings, and

music, who have interesting friends and discussions, who are curious and ask questions provide young children with all the intellectual stimulation they need. In such an environment, formal instruction would be like ordering a hamburger in a four-star restaurant.[7]

And, even though enrolling a child in an academically pushy preschool is undesirable, preschool itself can actually be an enriching experience. Activities involving age-appropriate group interactions, the manipulation and exploration of objects, and exposure to new experiences all create a wonderful learning environment for the young child. Sitting at a desk with a paper-and-pencil task or spending long periods of time sitting and listening to a teacher do not create the best possible learning environment for this age group. And remember the importance of play, the true work of childhood. Children who have learned to pour themselves fully and creatively into their play will one day be able to apply themselves fully and creatively to their work. As you look for a preschool for your child, investigate how well these needs of the preschooler are respected.

BUT MY CHILD REALLY IS GIFTED!

Perhaps you have been blessed with a truly gifted child. You want the best for your gifted child, the same as you do for your other children. Does this mean that you should try to get your child into a talented and gifted (TAG) program? Maybe. But then again, maybe not. Not all programs are the same, and the reasons children find themselves in such programs may have little to do with their needs. Sometimes the determining factor over whether or not a child enters a talented and gifted program can be the pushiness of the child's parents.

Programs for talented and gifted children can be found all over the country, and, as might be expected, some type

A parents eyeball these programs as potential crowns for parental crowing. The ingrained nature of parents in our culture to take the credit for their children's scholastic superiority was illustrated bluntly and unashamedly by a bumper sticker I spotted on the back of a car, which said something to the effect of: "My child is on the honor roll at Podunk Junior High." Whichever school it was that passed out those bumper stickers certainly did find a way to play on parental pride and familial enmeshment as a means of soliciting parental coercion of their children's success.

The sad fact is that both students and parents, as well as some teachers, often see programs for the talented and gifted as being a "reward" for doing superior work. At their inception, these programs were never meant to be used in such a manner. Nor were the programs developed because of concerns about providing sufficient education for intellectually advanced students. Funds were funneled into the education of talented and gifted children as a direct response to the Soviet Union's success with Sputnik.[8] Our country became concerned that our Cold War adversary would surpass us in military ability if we did not become better exploiters of our national talents. Thus it was military paranoia, not concerns for the needs of the gifted, that eventually resulted in the existence of TAG programs. Nevertheless, TAG programs have become an accepted part of school curriculum. Likewise, the programs are routinely hounded by parents and/or mainstream teachers to accept children, whether or not they or society would truly benefit from such placement.

But there is some question as to whether even the truly gifted child benefits from many TAG programs. TAG programs generally consist of taking children out of their mainstream classes for three to five hours a week. Research on pull-out programs has suggested that intellectually gifted children generally do not come out any further ahead after participating in such programs.[9]

In view of their limited benefits, perhaps we should also begin to take into account the potential undesired side effects of such programs. First, they label a subpopulation of children as being different from the others. In reality, all of us are different from everybody else in some respect. But TAG programs look at a specific difference and accentuate it as being something over which to segregate children. With all of the recent politicking surrounding giving minorities equal treatment, how is it that we are singling out people who are talented in academia? We certainly wouldn't stand for separating out blacks and giving them a different education on the basis of the color of their skin, for at least this one good reason: Separating children out attaches a stigma to them. Children who are learning-disabled are mainstreamed as much as possible, in part because of this reason. Segregation can be especially detrimental during the early teen years, when children begin the development of their adult autonomy by identifying with their peers. Pull-out programs give children the message that they do not fit in with their peers, and thus have the potential to interfere with this developmental task.

Second, it holds up academic achievement as being so important that children must be separated and given special treatment so that their talents will not go to waste. We do not take aside children who are great communicators, great humanitarians, or are superior in their sensitivity toward others in order to build up these talents. Yet, these skills are every bit as important to develop as intellectual skills, even more important in some life pursuits. Singling out academic ability gives children the message that achievement matters most—the beginning of an unbalanced attitude.

Third, children who are superior in intellect are usually aware that intellectualizing is their forte. Since their environment generally rewards it, they can easily learn to focus on activities and pastimes that accentuate it, perhaps to the detriment of social, emotional, and other aspects of child development. The last thing they need is to be separated out into a class that encourages them to become even more preoccupied with academics. If anything, they need activities that enhance interpersonal skills and draw their empathic and other sensing abilities into their daily living, and especially into their achievement pursuits.

Some TAG programs are sensitive to these realities and steer intellectually gifted children toward more balanced development. But many are not. The accelerated learning classroom is a typical example. If a child is gifted and is genuinely interested in a certain field, accelerated learning in that field may be the answer for him or her. But to inflict accelerated learning in all fields upon all gifted children just because they can handle it ignores the true needs of the intellectually gifted. Do we want our computer engineers to develop software that makes a true contribution to the needs of society? Or would we prefer that they spend their time developing "fritterware"—ego-involved software that is developed more for the engineer to prove he or she could get the computer to do it, rather than to help others with their needs?[10] A philosophy of living that includes social interest—valuing the needs and feelings of others—is much more likely to help the talented child apply his or her skills to society. Simply cramming in more information in an accelerated learning class will not do this, and it has the potential to make the child miss the whole point of developing his or her skills.

Another concern about TAG programs is their exclusive focus on intellectual prowess as being the entity that will ultimately aid society. Is this really so? Or is it *creativity* that is going to lead to finding a cure for AIDS, mechanisms for feeding the starving, and solutions for cleaning up the environment? Intelligence is not the same as creativity. Experts suggest that a certain level of intelligence is necessary for a person to be able to apply his or her creativity, but beyond a certain cut-off point, the level of intelligence becomes irrelevant.[11] Children are usually selected for TAG programs on the basis of grades and/or scores on intelligence tests. The relationship between creativity and academic aptitude may actually be nonexistent,[12] which brings into question the utility of using grades or achievement tests for the selection of the creatively gifted. True, there are probably more creative people represented by those who score at the high end of an intelligence test than at the low end, but what about all of the creative people who score at the moderate or moderately high levels of intelligence? Why would we exclude them in order to work with the highly intelligent, when we cannot say that only the highly intelligent are gifted with creativity?

The most comprehensive long-term study ever performed concerning intellectually gifted children looked at the comparative strengths and weaknesses of high and ordinary achievers.[13] While the intellectually gifted children were rated higher by teachers on numerous traits, they were rated lower than the ordinary group on mechanical ingenuity. Isn't this a form of creativity? One thing is certain: The higher achievers in this study did go on to get more education, get more prestigious jobs, earn a higher income, and enjoy better mental and physical health than did the ordinary group. This is to be expected, since intelligent people easily figure out the "rules" to any procedure and can be quite adept at sorting them out in ways that will help them succeed. But creativity comes from outside the norm; it is created. Someone who easily manipulates given relevant variables does not need to rely so much on creativity to meet needs as does the person with average intelligence. Could it be that we're barking up the wrong tree when we provide special training to the intellectually gifted as a means of enhancing our society, when the truly creative solutions are at least as likely to come from elsewhere?

TAG programs could do a tremendous service to society if they would work with the intellectually gifted under-achievers. How much more valuable these individuals would be to society if they could learn to channel their abilities into academic pursuits, rather than into becoming the future criminal geniuses. Unfortunately, underachievers generally do not make it into programs for the gifted, since superior achievement is often used as the criterion for admission.[14]

My hat goes off to the educators who are now wrestling with the development of TAG programs. They have their work cut out for them! It will be exciting to follow their progress, but in the meantime, we need to know what to do with our intellectually gifted children.

My advice is to begin by looking at how their learning can be enhanced at home, not with more formal education, but through methods from which all children can benefit. Give your children an "average expectable environment." Provide them with opportunities to learn, rather than forcing them into specific areas of learning. Make sure that you provide them with a model of balanced living. In other words, follow the plan for raising a healthy achiever.

Second, don't give up on TAG programs! Not all of them suffer from the pitfalls described earlier. Find out what the program is all about in your school district. Is it just accelerated learning? Does it focus on placing even more emphasis on developing intellectual skills to the exclusion of others? Does it provide new exposures and opportunities to learn, or is it just more rote memorization? How much attention will be given to the individual needs of your intellectually gifted child? Has the program been empirically evaluated to see if it really does enhance learning? If you are satisfied that the local TAG program has something to offer your child, go for it!

If you do not like the school's program, there are other routes you can take. Many private schools offer individualized programs for all of their students, regardless of their state of giftedness. A mainstream public school education can be enhanced through participation in activities offered by park and recreation districts, museums of science and industry, and other local organizations. If a child is progressing in his or her field beyond what the public school offers, look into the possibility of early enrollment in college courses, or check with local universities for the availability of private tutors in your child's field of excellence.

No matter which route you decide to take, remember that what you are guarding against is turning your superior achiever into a type A achiever. Help intellectually gifted children develop their talents, but guard against sacrificing their overall development in order to come out on top—the treadmill of the classic type A achiever. Our culture as it currently stands will encourage your intellectually gifted child to base his or her identity on that gift, just by the way our culture applauds it and rewards it. The most valuable thing we can do as parents is to help our children recognize that superior achieving, no matter how superior, can never be more than one corner of their character, and is only one small sample of the goodies of life we would like them to share in.

CULTURAL CHAINS OR CHANGE?

Can we change our culture? What are our chances for success at such an effort? Through individual efforts alone, probably not much. But when it comes to affecting cultural norms, I suspect we have more power collectively, as parents, than we have ever realized. The history of Western parenting habits illustrates our power.

During the early part of this century, there was an

excessive emphasis on the possibility of "spoiling" children. "Don't pick up the baby, or you'll spoil him," as well as "Let him cry—it's good for his lungs" were commonly heard as parents dealt with their children. Two world wars followed. The pendulum then swung, as the next generation of parents found the antithesis to such treatment in Benjamin Spock, who promoted fulfilling the need of babies to feel loved and supported. As parents overreacted in this direction, their children eventually made up the hippie generation. The pendulum swung back again with a return to emphasis on coercing good behavior, especially through reward, punishment, and demanding "correct" behavior above all else. The reaction of children to such sterile treatment seems to have promoted another new phenomenon: corporate raiders invading and dissecting businesses for financial gain, without any concern for the impact it will have on others.

Whether or not the correlations between childrearing practices and historical events are illusory, perhaps it is time for the pendulum to be stilled. Surely we can now recognize that any one childrearing policy taken to the extreme is absurd. Childrearing is certainly easier if we go by one concept, one book, or one "guru." And all childrearing techniques have their merit when used in appropriate situations. But just because you have a well-functioning hammer does not mean that everything is a nail. The time has come for us to integrate all that science and eons of parenting experience have taught us and come out with a whole that meets the needs of today's children.

In my view, the key will undoubtedly involve finding a balance. Yes, discipline children, encourage them, guide them, help them to be all they can be. But we cannot sacrifice their souls in the process. Let our discipline show them that we love them, not through the coercion-age cop-out of "I spank you because I love you," but instead by including an appeal to their inner empathic spirits, the part of them that can recognize and experience the discomfort or joy that their actions can bring upon others. Let our encouragement be child-centered, rather than centered on what we would like our children to be or how we would like to make them more like us. Let our guidance expand their opportunities, rather than narrow them to that with which we ourselves feel safe.

We all can succeed in simply being the people we are; none of us can succeed in being the people others wish we were. Will our next generation be able to appreciate this reality?

Chapter Eight

Epilogue

Jimmy D. watched as Joey pedaled out of sight. He felt a stirring within him, not something he could readily identify, but a vague tugging at his heart strings. He looked down at the bare strip running down the alyssum bed.

"Joanna will have this filled in with transplants in no time," he thought out loud.

But that was not it. He sat on the grass and looked up at the clouds rolling in from the west.

"Rain's coming soon," he predicted. As the sky darkened and a few isolated drops splattered onto his face, he pondered this feeling, this sense that something was not right.

"Joey's gonna get soaked in this one," he realized. He got up and climbed into the four-wheel drive and drove off to find Joey. Scanning the length of the neighborhood, he spotted Joey's bike at the park. As he pulled up into the parking lot, he could see the silhouette of his son, slouching at the top of the jungle gym.

"Better get your bike home," he called to Joey as he approached. "We don't want it to get rusted out."

"I don't care about any stupid bike," Joey muttered.

"What do you mean you don't care about it? That's one of the best bikes money can buy. When I was a kid I had to work for months to be able to afford. . . . " Jimmy D. paused. *When I was a kid.*

"What do you care anyway?" yelled Joey. "It's not yours. All you care about is *your* stupid yard and *your* stupid house and *your* stupid car and. . . . "

"That's enough!"

"You can say that again."

Jimmy D. recognized that once again they were in their usual stand-off: Joey angry, sulking and uncooperative, and Jimmy D. fuming. "Why doesn't this ever work out?" he thought. *You never get anything right.*

The wind was picking up, and the scattered raindrops had progressed to a steady sprinkle.

"Isn't it getting a little cold up there?" Jimmy D. asked.

"No," Joey lied.

Jimmy D.'s impatience caught up with him. "Come on, Joey, let's go! I'm getting all wet."

"Well, we certainly wouldn't want anybody to see that."

"Look, what makes you think a punk like you. . . . " *A punk like you.*

"That's right, Dad, now let's try some name-calling." *You never get anything right.*

"I won't stand for this!" Jimmy D. bellowed. "I took enough of this sort of bull when I was a kid. The least you could do right now is show a little bit of respect and common decency and. . . . " *When I was a kid.*

"How about me, Dad? Don't I deserve any respect? Who do you think did everything at home while you were lying around in the hospital? Isn't anything I do good enough?" *Nothing I do is good enough.*

"Good enough. . . . " Jimmy D. began to perceive what the stirring had meant, what had driven him to find Joey and bring him home. He looked down and smiled, a bittersweet, tearful smile, for feelings he still wasn't sure he understood.

"You gave it your best shot, Joey. I guess we can't expect any more of ourselves than that."

Joey did not know how to respond. By now the rain was pouring steadily, and as Jimmy D. had predicted, they were getting soaked.

"Come on, let's go home," said Jimmy D.

Joey hesitated, then slowly slid down the bars and walked toward his bike. He rode on ahead, while Jimmy D. followed behind. Jimmy D., though emotionally drained, sensed a peculiar strength within him.

"What is this?" he struggled. "What am I finding in Joey and myself that has me so shaken?"

Jimmy D. did not find quick, easy answers to his questions. However, it did not take long for him and Joey to fall back into their usual pattern of angry interacting. At his next physician's visit, he mentioned in passing the incident in the park, and the doctor suggested that maybe this sort of thing might be something Jimmy D. would want to explore with a counselor. Jimmy D. balked. "Counselors! Shrinks! What sort of a wimp do I look like?"

His physician gave him the name of a family therapist anyway. Despite his nonchalant attitude, Jimmy D. could not lay to rest the idea of getting therapy. He had experienced something different and freeing that day in the park with Joey, and he wanted more of it. But being able to get it only with somebody else's help? That would be a threat to his basic competency!

Threat or no threat, he began to realize that while he had been preoccupied with his career, his family life had been crumbling around him. As the children had been growing older, Joanna had been filling her time with more and more activities away from home. And as the children grew older, they spent more time at their friends' houses than they did at home; and when they were home, they generally avoided Jimmy D. A sense of panic filled him, as he watched his family drifting away during a time when he was beginning to realize that "family" might mean something more than an entity to provide for. Begrudgingly, he made himself contact the family therapist.

Thus marked the beginning of a long journey for Jimmy D. His whole family eventually attended the sessions. Joanna was confused about it at first, not really understanding what she was there for. Janet feared the sessions, often worrying about what new situation might erupt between Joey and her dad. Joey understood that his dad wanted to work on their relationship, but didn't see the point in the sessions. He called the therapist "medicine man" and usually made fun of his comments and interventions. A few months after therapy started Joey was gone anyway, as he began his college career in a distant town.

In spite of Joey's apparent noncompliance with therapy, it was not a waste of time for him. He saw his father placing a value on relationships that was worth swallowing his pride for. He had been made aware that there were other ways of interacting than those his father had modeled. He learned that his behavior can affect his health. And most of all, he saw his father model his vulnerability, being willing to show that he was not perfect; yet, the roof did not fall in, and his worth continued to be validated by the therapist.

Ten years have passed. Joey and his wife, Heather, are sitting on their veranda and watching their children, David and Roseanne, run through the sprinkler. It's one of those warm steamy summer days, when all you want to do is lean back, sip your lemonade, listen to the gentle wind in the tree tops, and enjoy the hothouse atmosphere of fragrant flowers and buzzing insects. The shouts and the laughter of the children add bell-like peals to the sultry summer sounds.

David decides to help with watering the lawn and moves

the sprinkler to the other side of the yard. As he shows his parents his latest new tricks in sprinkler-jumping, he does not see that the new sprinkler position is also liberally watering the inside of Joey's convertible.

"Oh, no!" groans Joey as he assesses the damage. David stands by his mother, looking ashamed and fearing rejection. Joey looks down at his son, whose young brown eyes are pooling over with tears of regret. Joey sighs.

"It's okay, sport. Everybody makes mistakes. We can't expect you to do any more than your best, right?"

David runs up and gives his dad a hug. "Watch this, Dad!" he says. "This time I'll really show you. . . . "

Aren't happy endings wonderful? Joey's family functioning seems drastically different from what he learned from his family of origin, doesn't it? However, it is not likely that Joey's story has progressed so differently just due to chance. Somewhere in the course of the intervening years he must have had continuing influences that guided him toward this style of interacting, which is so different from the one dictated by his family legacy. Perhaps he learned through the "school of hard knocks"—failed relationships, lost job opportunities, or damaged health. Maybe in college he fell in with a different crowd, one that lived a more caring, balanced life-style. Joey may have read up on the latest type A research and decided he wanted to work toward something better for himself and his family. Or maybe Joey's brief therapy experience affected him in a way that lead to his eventual decision to get more therapy on his own. We can only speculate. Whatever the cause of the change, we can be certain that it did not come without a lot of pain, soul searching, and hard work.

But many will benefit from Joey's courageous efforts. Joey himself will have a better chance of being healthier, happier, and more productive than he ever could have been as a type A achiever. His co-workers will be more likely to be successful as well, as Joey channels his social interest into cooperative efforts with others. They will be more likely to know him as a friend, rather than as a hostile competitor. Heather will have a husband who is more likely to be sensitive to her needs, supportive of her own efforts and desires, and willing to make time for their relationship. Likewise, she will have fewer worries about becoming an early widow!

David and Roseanne will receive the greatest benefits of all. They will have a truly involved father, not just a figurehead who makes token appearances, long enough to bark orders and enforce coercive discipline, and then be on his way. In Joey they will observe a model of healthy achieving: a balanced life-style, a desire to relate to others rather than control them, an optimistic attitude toward the world, and a realistic, less fearful view of challenge. Most of all, they will be more likely to feel loved and accepted, validated in their worth no matter how they may succeed or fail, and unfettered in their ability to reach out and try new things. In other words, they are the lucky inhabiters of an "average expectable environment."

And the benefits will not stop with David and Roseanne. The model of parenting they receive will be remembered when they raise their own children, who will also benefit. No matter which temperament those children are born with or how the current state of Western culture affects them, the pattern of parenting initiated by Jimmy D. and built upon by Joey is likely to persevere, encouraging the new generation's chances of becoming healthy achievers.

What greater gift could we give to our families? The proverbial gift that keeps on giving! If you still have not decided whether you want to do anything about your type A functioning, ask yourself this: If today were your last day on earth, would you really want to spend it in a pit of pessimism? Or how about stewing all day over some minor failure or emotional slight? Or feeling guilty over having been excessively harsh with a family member? Or worrying that someone will notice some minor imperfection in one of your pursuits? Or being concerned that the other guy is going to get ahead of you? Is this how you would spend your time, knowing that your life would end at nightfall?

In closing, I would like to offer some reminders for those of you who are using this book as a guide for familial change.

1. Remember that you are not going to change things overnight. Family patterns develop over many generations. But as the story of Joey and Jimmy D. shows, change *can* come. Have patience with the time it takes to make a true difference.

2. Don't expect to change everything. Pick a few aspects of your type A relating or parenting that you feel you have the best chance of altering and invest your full efforts into improving them. You can build on your progress as time passes.

3. Continue to value those aspects of your family functioning that are already in good shape. Just because you now recognize dysfunctional relating in your family system does not mean that your family is entirely dysfunctional. Build on the family strengths that already exist.

4. Be aware that your desire to change may not be easily accepted by other family members. Just as Joey did not know how to react to Jimmy D.'s changed tactics, so also your family members may not know what to do with you if you are changing your style from hyperaggressive to assertive, critical to supportive, or ever-absent to ever-present. Give them time to adjust, and enlist the support of your family as you adjust yourself.

5. Do not confuse changing your behavior with changing your inborn temperament. You may always internally react strongly to frustrating situations. This continued internal presence does not mean that you have not become successful in managing it after it is sensed.

6. Do not expect your extended family to be different just because you have changed. Your father may continue to reject your long distance phone calls because of the "waste" of your money, not realizing that the waste of the relationship is the true tragedy. You can always hope that your own changes will rub off on others, but do not set your hopes inordinately high. Learn to accept the things that you cannot change.

7. Above all, remember that your goal is to live a balanced, full life. Don't let therapy for type A behavior take over your life in the same way that your type A functioning can crowd out living. Introduce change, experiment with it, explore it, and revel in its benefits. But protect and cherish a focus on filling your days with moments that are gratifying, rather than counting the notches of success that your living might bring.

Notes

Chapter Two   The Unhealthy Achiever

1. See M. Friedman and D. Ulmer, *Treating Type A Behavior—and Your Heart* (New York: Fawcett Crest, 1984).

2. See C. Thoresen and J. Pattillo, "Exploring the Type A Behavior Pattern in Children and Adolescents." To appear in B. K. Houston and C. R. Snyder, eds., *Type A Behavior Pattern: Current Trends and Future Directions* (New York: John Wiley, in press).

3. See K. A. Matthews and S. A. Haynes, "Type A Behavior Pattern and Coronary Disease Risk: Update and Critical Evaluation," *American Journal of Epidemiology* 123 (1986): 923-60.

4. See Friedman and Ulmer, *Treating Type A Behavior—and Your Heart*.

Chapter Three   Type A Parent—Type A Child

1. See J. Kagan, "Temperamental Contributions to Social Behavior," *American Psychologist* 44 (1989): 668-74.

2. Ibid.

3. See H. Hartmann, *Ego Psychology and the Problem of Adaptation* (New York: International Universities Press, 1958).

Chapter Four   Becoming a Healthy Achiever

1. Shirley Gould, *The Challenge of Achievement* (New York: Hawthorne Books, 1978).

2. Ibid., p. 117.

3. See Friedman and Ulmer, *Treating Type A Behavior—and Your Heart*, chapter 11.

4. I would like to thank Dennis Pinheiro for sharing this story with me.

Chapter Five   Healing the Parent

1. Gerald Kranzler, *You Can Change How You Feel: A Rational-Emotive Approach* (Eugene, Ore.: RETC Press, 1974).

2. See R. Novaco, "The Cognitive Regulation of Anger and Stress." In P. Kendall and S. Hollon, eds., *Cognitive-behavioral Interventions: Theory, Research, and Procedures* (New York: Academic Press, 1979).

3. See David Burns, *Feeling Good: The New Mood Therapy* (New York: Signet, 1980) and Albert Ellis and Robert Harper, *A New Guide to Rational Living* (Hollywood, Calif.: Wilshire Book Company, 1975).

4. See R. Alberti and M. Emmons, *Your Perfect Right: A Guide to Assertive Behavior* (San Luis Obispo, Calif.: Impact Publishers, 1978).

5. Ibid.

6. Redford Williams, *The Trusting Heart: Great News About Type A Behavior* (New York: Times Books, 1989).

7. Ibid., chapter 11.

8. See Friedman and Ulmer, *Treating Type A Behavior—and Your Heart*, pp. 266-71.

9. See Herbert Benson, *The Relaxation Response* (New York: Avon, 1975).

10. See Joan Borysenko, *Minding the Body, Mending the Mind* (Reading, Mass.: Addison-Wesley, 1987).

11. See Eugene Gendlin, *Focusing* (New York: Bantam Books, 1981).

12. H. Ansbacher and R. Ansbacher, *The Individual Psychology of Alfred Adler: A Systematic Presentation in Selections from His Writings* (New York: Harper & Row, 1956), p. 134.

13. Harold Kushner, *When All You've Ever Wanted Isn't Enough: The Search for a Life That Matters* (New York: Pocket Books, 1986), pp. 142-43.

Chapter Six   Helping the Child

1. See J. Kagan, "Temperamental Contributions to Social Behavior," *American Psychologist* 44 (1989): 665-74; and J. Kagan, *The Power and Limitations of Parents* (Austin, Tex.: University of Texas Press, 1986).

2. Ibid.

3. See Laurel Hughes, *How to Raise Good Children: Encouraging Moral Growth* (Nashville: Abingdon Press, 1988).

4. See Bob Keeshan, *Growing Up Happy: Captain Kangaroo Tells Yesterday's Children How to Nurture Their Own* (New York: Doubleday, 1989), pp. 42-43.

Chapter Seven   Western Culture and Childrearing

1. See E. Zaretsky, *Capitalism, the Family, and Personal Life* (New York: Harper & Row, 1976).

2. See Kagan, *The Power and Limitations of Parents.*

3. James Uphoff, as quoted in A. Chaplin, "The Superbaby Syndrome," *The Oregonian* (November 10, 1987): D20.

4. Ibid.

5. Ibid.

6. James Uphoff, June Gilmore, and Rosemarie Huber, *Summer Children: Ready or Not for School* (Middletown, Ohio: J & J Publishing Co., 1986).

7. David Elkind, *The Hurried Child: Growing Up Too Fast Too Soon* (Reading, Mass.: Addison-Wesley, 1981), pp. 65-66.

8. See L. Bruner, *The Process of Education* (Cambridge, Mass.: Harvard University Press, 1960).

9. See J. Van Tassel-Baska, "The Ineffectiveness of the Pull-out Program Model in Gifted Education: A Minority Perspective," *Journal for the Education of the Gifted* 10 (1987): 255-64.

10. I would like to thank my brother, Mark Chamberlain, for sharing with me the concept of "fritterware," so named because both the developer and the user end up frittering away a lot of time and effort with it.

11. See J. Sattler, *Assessment of Children's Intelligence and Social Abilities,* 2nd ed. (Boston: Allyn & Bacon, 1982), p. 440.

12. See J. Holland, "Creative and Academic Performance Among Talented Adolescents," *Journal of Educational Psychology* 52 (1961): 136-47.

13. See L. Terman and M. Oden, *The Gifted Group at Midlife* (Stanford, Calif.: University Press, 1959).

14. See J. Gallagher, "National Agenda for Educating Gifted Students: Statement of Priorities," *Exceptional Children* 55 (1988): 107-14.

Index

Accelerated learning, 123
Achievement: by child, 40, 103
  healthy, 37, 51-55, 66
  philosophy of, 58
  and identity, 76
  as a measure of worth, 30, 44,
    46, 48, 49-50, 56, 57, 59, 86-87,
    88
  rewarded by type A parents, 48,
    97
  rewarded by Western culture,
    24, 46, 50, 54, 126
Achievement orientation, 27-28
  healthy, 27-28
  type A parents modeling, 47
Affection: conditional, by type A
    parent, 40, 97
  difficulty expressing, to chil-
    dren, 31, 40, 44
  expression of by children, 101-2
  lack of, felt by type A person,
    30-31
Anger management, 76-79
Antisocial behavior, children's,
    45, 117
Assertiveness, 79-81, 82, 96, 98
Attitude. *See* Philosophy of life
"Average expectable environ-
    ment," 43-45, 116-17, 125,
    134

Balanced life-style, 54-55, 89, 136
  lack of in type A person, 57

promoting in children, 100-104,
    107, 125
Beliefs: challenging, 73-74, 78-79
  dysfunctional, 54, 57, 74-79
  feelings caused by, 60-61
  of the healthy achiever, 64-66,
    73-74
  of the type A person, 62-64,
    72-73
Benson, H., 89
Blood pressure, high, 33, 73, 104
Borysenko, J., 89

Cardiovascular disease, 23-24, 28-
    29, 71, 78
  avoiding, 83-85
  and type A behavior, 33-34, 36,
    38, 66
Competitiveness: healthy, 27, 37
  and low self-esteem, 30
  and the monkey troop, 67-68
  and parenting, 40, 102, 104
  as a type A characteristic, 26, 27,
    28, 31-32, 34, 59
  type A parents modeling, 47
Creativity, 123-25
Criticism: of children by type A
    parents, 40, 43-44, 48, 97, 98,
    100, 101, 107
  fear of, by children, 46
  modeled by type A parents, 47
  rewarded by type A parents, 48
  as a type A behavior, 26, 31

Decision-making: building children's skills at, 97-98, 99, 102, 107
by the healthy achiever, 52-53
by the type A achiever, 56
Diaphragmatic breathing, 72, 96
Discipline, child, 99-100, 101, 126-28
Depression, in children, 46
Dominating: modeled by type A parents, 47
and parenting, 40, 44, 98, 101, 103-4, 105, 107
as a type A characteristic, 30, 57, 79, 101

Educational toys, 116-17
Elkind, David, 119-20
Empathy: promoting in children, 100-101, 123
healthy achiever's capacity for, 58
impaired ability for in type A person, 31-32, 59
and social interest, 90-91
type A parents for child's criticalness, 48
Enmeshment between type A parent and child, 41, 49, 121
Enrollment, early, 116-18
Exercise, 27, 34, 84-85

Fanaticism, 26, 84
Feelings: and behavioral choices, 61, 62-66
beliefs lead to, 60, 62-66
healing, 72-76
Forgiveness, 82-83
Free-floating hostility: developing in children, 42-45
healing, 76-79
modeled by type A parents, 47
and parenting, 39
as a product of feeling unloved, 30-31
as a type A characteristic, 26, 28
Friedman, M., 24, 32-33, 66, 91

Gendlin, E., 90
Goal orientation, 25, 26, 35, 47, 53, 68-69, 88, 92, 100, 105-6
Gould, Shirley, 51, 54

Heart. *See* Cardiovascular disease
Hurry sickness, 24, 25
and parenting, 39, 48
Hyperaggressiveness, 25-26
healing, 79-81
modeled by type A parents, 47
and parenting, 39

Identity: and achievement, 76
cultural influences on, 114-15, 126
encouraging children's sense of, 97
of the healthy achiever, 52
personal, 74-76
of the type A person, 59
Impatience, 25, 96
Industry, role of in childrearing, 113-15
Interpersonal relationships: children's, 102, 106, 118, 123
healing of the type A person, 76-83
and healthy achievers, 52-55
importance of, 69
modeled by type A parents, 47
type A person's difficulties with, 31-32, 57, 59, 101, 104
Intelligence, 123-24

Kushner, Harold, 92-93

Laughter, 85
Learning: and the healthy achiever, 53
modeling and, 46-47
and the type A achiever, 56
type A behavior, 45-50

Migraine headaches, 33

Meditation. *See* Relaxation: techniques
Modeling: effect of on children 46-47, 71
by type A parents 47-48
Multiple activities. *See* Time urgency

Norepinephrine, 33

Optimism, experienced by healthy achiever, 54
Overachieving, 23, 47, 55, 122-23

Pessimism, 45, 47, 66, 81-83, 86
Philosophy of life: effect of, on feelings and behavior, 60-67
of the healthy achiever, 58, 64-66, 70, 93, 107
of the type A achiever, 56, 59, 62-64, 6
Potential, children's, 105
Power, preoccupation with, 32, 41, 44, 101
Preschool, 116, 120

Relaxation: importance of, 55, 85, 104
techniques, 84, 88-90
Rewards: for children making efforts, 97
for children repeating behaviors, 47
as discipline, 101, 127
TAG programs as, 121
type A parents providing for achievement, 48, 97, 105
for child's being critical of others, 48
Western culture providing for achievement, 46, 122
Roles. *See* Identity
Rubber-band technique, 73, 81, 96

Science, presuppositions of, 87
Segregation, 120

Self-acceptance: encouraging children's sense of, 96-97
experienced by the healthy achiever, 52, 53-54, 58
Self-actualization, 42-44
Self-confidence. *See* Self-esteem
Self-esteem: good promoting in children, 96-100
of the healthy achiever, 52, 53, 58, 76
low in children starting school early, 117, 118
coping strategies used by children for, 45-46
developing in children, 38-42, 76, 105
of the type A person, 29-31, 55, 59
as opposed to self-acceptance, 58
and parenting ability, 115-16
Self-respect. *See* Self-esteem
Self-sufficience: of the healthy achiever, 52
type A achiever's lack of, 56
Self-worth. *See* Self-esteem
Smoking, 84
Social interest, 54-55, 57, 80, 90-91, 123, 133-34
Spirituality: Buddhist, 85-86, 91
Confucian, 91
Judeo-Christian, 88-89, 91, 92-93
healing, 85-93
lack of in type A, 34-35
Spock, Benjamin, 127
Status insecurity, 29-30, 119
developing in children, 38-42
Stress: in children, 117
effect on the body of, 32-33
managing, 84
Success. *See* Achievement
"Superbaby" syndrome, 116-17

TAG programs, 120-26
Talents, children's, 106, 119-26

Temperament, inborn, 41-42, 43, 95-96, 134, 135
Thoughts. *See* Beliefs
Thought-stopping, 73, 77, 82, 96
Time urgency: modeled by type A parents, 47-48
  and parenting, 39, 43, 49;
  as a type A characteristic, 28, 30
Trust, 81-83

"Unconditional positive regard," 44, 97
Underachievers, 46, 125
Uphoff, J., 117-18

Western culture, 114-28, 134
  rewarding type A behavior, 46, 50
  and type A characteristics, 24